D. Caroline Coile, Ph.D.

Miniature Pinschers

Everything about Purchase, Care, Nutrition,
Breeding, Behavior, and Training

With 34 Color Photographs

Illustrations by Michele Earle-Bridges

BARRON'S

Acknowledgments

The information contained in this book comes from a variety of sources: breeders, original research, scientific articles, veterinary journals, and a library of dog books. But by far my most heartfelt gratitude must go to my most demanding teachers, who have taught me the skills of both home repair and dog repair, allowed ample testing opportunities for behavioral problem cures, and whetted my curiosity (and carpets) about everything canine for the past 20 years: Baha, Khyber, Tundra, Kara, Hypatia, Savannah, Sissy, Dixie, Bobby, Kitty, Jeepers, Bean-Boy, Junior, Khyzi, Wolfman, and Stinky.

All inquiries should be addressed to:
Barron's Educational Series, Inc.
250 Wireless Boulevard
Hauppauge, NY 11788

ISBN-13: 978-0-8120-9346-9
ISBN-10: 0-8120-9346-1

Library of Congress Catalog Card No. 95-19007

Library of Congress Cataloging-in-Publication Data
Coile, D. Caroline.
    Miniature pinschers : everything about purchase, care, nutrition, breeding, behavior, and training with color photos. / D. Caroline Coile ; drawings by Michele Earle-Bridges.
        p. cm. — (A Complete pet owner's manual)
    Includes bibliographical references (p.   ) and index.
        ISBN 0-8120-9346-1
        1. Miniature pinschers. I. Title. II. Series.
SF429.M56C65   1996
636.7′6—dc20   95-19007
                                                CIP

Printed in China

23 22 21 20 19 18 17

About the Author

Caroline Coile is an award-winning author who has written articles about dogs for both scientific and lay publications. She holds a Ph.D. in the field of neuroscience and behavior, with special interests in canine sensory systems, genetics, and behavior. Her own dogs have been nationally ranked in conformation, obedience, and field-trial competition.

Photo Credits:

Barbara Augello: front cover, pages 53, 80 left; Caroline Coile: page 12 top; Donna Coss: inside front cover, inside back cover, back cover, pages 12 bottom, 33, 68, 72, 77, 80 right; Georgette Curran: page 36 right; Robert Dawes: pages 13 top; Joe and Helen Gloyd: page 13 bottom, 20; Earl Graham Studios: page 81; Susan Green: pages 8, 9, 24, 25, 28, 29, 32, 40, 49, 60, 73, 76; Aaron Norman: pages 37, 48; Noren Trotman: page 17; Toni Tucker: pages 4, 36 left, 65, 84, 85.

Important Note

This pet owner's guide tells the reader how to buy and care for a miniature pinscher. The author and the publisher consider it important to point out that the advice given in the book is meant primarily for normally developed puppies from a good breeder— that is, dogs of excellent physical health and good character.

Anyone who adopts a fully grown dog should be aware that the animal has already formed its basic impressions of human beings. The new owner should watch the animal carefully, including its behavior toward humans, and should meet the previous owner. If the dog comes from a shelter, it may be possible to get some information on the dog's background and peculiarities there. There are dogs that, as a result of bad experiences with humans, behave in an unnatural manner or may even bite. Only people that have experience with dogs should take in such animals.

Caution is further advised in the association of children with dogs, in meeting with other dogs, and in exercising the dog without a leash.

Even well-behaved and carefully supervised dogs sometimes do damage to someone else's property or cause accidents. It is therefore in the owner's interest to be adequately insured against such eventualities, and we strongly urge all dog owners to purchase a liability policy that covers their dog.

Contents

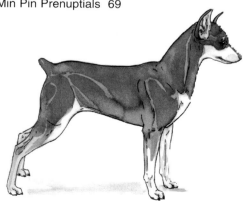

Preface

The miniature pinscher is one of a kind. Rambunctious, impetuous, and oh so very busy, the miniature pinscher (more affectionately known as the Min Pin) is the dog world's answer to the perpetual motion machine. Not surprisingly, Min Pin owners are themselves a unique breed. If you are contemplating joining their ranks, this is your invitation to explore life with a Min Pin before you take the plunge. And if you are lucky enough to already be one of the royal subjects of this "king of toys," then this is your opportunity to further delve into the many unique aspects of Min Pin health, training, behavior, genetics, and care.

The Min Pin is definitely not for everyone. Such a special and unique breed requires a special and unique owner. But when dog and owner find each other, the combination is magic. Perhaps the Min Pin can work its magic with you.

D. Caroline Coile, Ph.D.

The Miniature Pinscher: the king of the toys.

4

Understanding the Miniature Pinscher

The Min Pin's Past

The miniature pinscher is not a miniature version of the Doberman pinscher.

In fact, the miniature pinscher is the older of the two breeds. Although the two breeds resemble each other superficially, that resemblance probably stems in part from their common relation to the German pinscher, an older yet now comparatively rare breed intermediate in size between the two. But to understand the Min Pin of today, it is necessary to first take a step back in time.

The miniature pinscher is both an ancient and a modern breed. Ancient because it descends from terrier-type dogs indigenous to Germany for many centuries, but modern because its present form is derived from the purposeful interbreeding of several breeds in the early nineteenth century.

The ancient terriers came in both medium and small sizes, and in both smooth and wire (and sometimes long) coats. These feisty dogs were adept at dispatching vermin, and even today their descendants are apt and fearless hunters. Because of the emphasis upon function, the sizes and coat types were commonly interbred as late as the eighteenth century. However, as interest in specialized pure breeds grew, the types eventually were separated and became the foundation for many of the modern-day breeds, including the miniature pinscher.

Clues about the miniature pinscher's development are scarce, but it is note-worthy that as early as 1640 a small cat-sized red dog, fine boned and with prick ears, is depicted in a painting of a peasant family. It is likely that this represents one of the small short-haired terriers rather than a distinct breed, however. Later paintings from the 1800s include dogs of distinctly miniature pinscher type.

Although it cannot be documented, it is believed that the miniature pin-scher resulted from the crossing of the small short-haired terrier with the dachshund and the Italian greyhound. Many of the traits of these original breeds can be seen in today's miniature pinschers: the feistiness, strong body structure, and black and tan coloration of the German pinscher; the fearlessness and clear red coloration of the dachshund; and the playfulness, elegance, and lithe movement of the Italian greyhound. But there is no accounting for the sheer energy level and inquisitive nature of today's miniature pinschers!

These little German spitfires were developed into a distinct breed, the "reh pinscher," in the early 1800s. The reh is a small red German deer (or roe deer), which the little dog was thought to resemble, and pinscher simply means terrier, which is an accurate reflection of its feisty ancestry.

German breeds of dog have earned the reputation of being some of the most finely bred dogs in the world. Their standards of perfection are exacting, and their criteria for breeding are stringent. The reh pinscher was no exception. The early (late 1800s) emphasis upon breeding the tiniest miniature pinscher, with no regard for grace or soundness of movement or body, threatened to result in a race of diminutive cripples with bulging eyes. Luckily this trend was reversed, so that by the time the breed was awarded official breed recognition in 1895, the foundation for the elegant, agile, strong-bodied miniature pinschers as they are known today was clearly discernible.

These modern-type miniature pinschers quickly became one of the most popular and well-developed show dogs in pre-World War I Germany, but following the war there the German Min Pin experienced a plunge in both numbers and quality. Fortunately the breed had been exported and was gaining fans abroad, including in America, where it received American Kennel

Despite appearances, the miniature pinscher is not a bred down Doberman pinscher.

Club (AKC) recognition in 1929 as a member of the toy group.

Since that time, the miniature pinscher has slowly accumulated an almost fanatically loyal following. With careful breeding, the breed has become more elegant, refined, and graceful, without sacrificing its strength and vitality. Today's Min Pin is lively, animated, feisty, and independent. Its sleek lines, lithe and supple body, and high-stepping hackney prance make it an eye-catcher in any crowd. One look at a Min Pin surveying its domain and there is no question why it has been dubbed the "king of toys."

Miniature pinschers have long been a favorite of dog show exhibitors. With their natural "look-at-me" attitude, they are show dogs par excellence. But more recently, they have attracted the attention of families interested only in having an elegant showstopper in their own home. Pet owners have discovered that the miniature pinscher can be an alert watchdog, a lively companion, and an untiring clown.

But as the Min Pin grows in popularity, many people are drawn to the breed without fully understanding the minuses as well as the pluses of having a whirling dervish in their homes. Increased popularity brings with it a host of uncaring and unknowing breeders who perpetuate incorrect Min Pin type, poor health, and poor temperaments. Ethical breeders are under increased pressure to place their puppies with great care in order to preserve and protect this unique breed. They know that it takes a special person to fully appreciate these special dogs—are you such a person?

The Min Pin Yen

So you think you want a miniature pinscher: a lively, loving, playful, svelte, loyal, obedient, protective, wonderful dog that will make Lassie and Rin-Tin-Tin look like canine underachievers. And you want it now. You want to get in the car and head to Wonderpups, Inc., and surprise the family with a dog that plays like a pup but is miraculously trained like an adult. Stop. Put your checkbook away and your thinking cap on.

A dog, especially a Min Pin, is not an impulse item. Dogs make wonderful pets in part because they are almost childlike in their dependence upon their human families, and because they bond so deeply with them. Don't get a dog on a trial basis. If you tire of your dog and think it won't be bothered when you cast it aside, think again. After you have used up its irresistibly cute puppy months, there will be few people lining up to offer it a new home.

Can you make the commitment of time every day, every *single* day, for the next 10 to 15 years of your life, to feed, exercise, train, and love this dependent being? Can you make the financial commitment? The cost of the dog is the least of your worries (and actually, considering the number of years you will have it, a bargain). But food, equipment, boarding, and vet bills can be high. Get on the phone right now, call several veterinary clinics in your area, and ask the prices for office visits, a series of puppy vaccinations, deworming, ear cropping, yearly checkups, neutering or spaying, emergency clinic visits, and monthly heartworm prevention. There are some companies offering doggy health insurance, but it's not cheap either. But what about making money in dogs? There is no doubt that dogs are a lucrative business—for the pet food industry, pet supply stores, boarding kennels, veterinarians—in short, everybody you will be paying. But if you plan to make money with your own dogs, the best business decision you can make is to not even get the first one, because it's all in the red after that.

Does everybody in the family feel the same way about your plan? Dogs make very poor surprise gifts. All family members should be encouraged to express their concerns now. Getting a dog will involve some sacrifice from everyone at home, whether it be losing a favorite shoe, a night's uninterrupted sleep, or the freedom to take a trip around the world. It is very difficult to accept such sacrifices if the puppy was not wanted in the first place. A Min Pin may be little, but it will make sure it is noticed!

Never get a dog just for the children. No matter how sincere the promises to take care of the puppy might be at the time, Mom or Dad will ultimately end up doing most of the work. It is not fair to the pup to use its missed dinner as a lesson to teach Junior the meaning of responsibility.

What do you want in a dog? Companionship? Hunting? Protection? Showing? A way to meet people? What don't you want in a dog? Shedding? Aggressiveness? Shyness? Don't choose a breed

In many ways the miniature pinscher resembles a tiny deer.

Even Min Pins sleep.

you have the temperament and lifestyle to appreciate the Min Pin's temperament and lifestyle. Because the Min Pin is not going to change.

Far too often dogs are acquired with the idea that all breeds act the same. They don't. The very reason that different breeds were initially created stemmed from differences in behavior, not looks. Dogs were selected for their propensity to trail, point, retrieve, herd, protect, or even cuddle, with physical attributes often secondary to behavioral. Min Pins are from stock created to seek and destroy rats, a task that required vigilance, courage, and tenacity. Don't get a miniature pinscher and ask it to act like a collie, retriever, or even a full-size Doberman. It's just not in its genes.

So what is in the Min Pin's genes? First of all, recall that miniature pinschers are *not* miniature Doberman pinschers. Despite their appearance, they were not bred down from the larger breed. They are related, and they do share some temperament features, but they differ in as many ways as they are similar. There are individual differences, but the typical Min Pin is an ultralively, bold, inquisitive, energetic, bright, comical, quick-witted dog, full of self-confidence and pride, and always on the lookout for trouble!

Min Pins respond to affection, but are not overly demonstrative; they tend to attach themselves to one member of the family to the exclusion of others. Often Min Pins not only consider themselves to be a part of the family, but they will try to be the head of it! These little Napoleons do sometimes have a problem in accepting a human as their leader, and dominance struggles are a reported problem.

The Min Pin is a big dog in a little body. If the good manners that are expected of big dogs are also expected of this little big dog, then it can be a well-mannered family

because your neighbor has one, or it was the star of a recent movie, or it's the current rage, or just because it looks neat. Carefully decide what attributes you want in a dog, and what you don't want; with over 150 recognized breeds in the United States alone, there's very likely a breed out there with your name on it. Maybe it's the miniature pinscher.

The Inimitable Min Pin— Is It for You?

Temperament

Most people are initially attracted to a breed because of its looks, and the dapper little Min Pin is undeniably stunning. No breed of dog—absolutely *no* breed—can compete with the Min Pin when it comes to strutting, prancing, and standing at attention. But have you ever seen a Min Pin at rest? Yes, they do sleep, but most Min Pins have to fit sleep into a very busy calendar. Many people find this constant activity to be one of the most enchanting and entertaining attributes of the breed; others find it unnerving or even annoying. It is best to find out early if member. A spoiled Min Pin is apt to become the family tyrant, so it requires a firm (but gentle) hand and some obedience training. Often headstrong, its diminutive size, nonetheless, makes any harsh corrections inadvisable.

Min Pins are excellent watchdogs, and although they will try to be a formidable protection dog, their size makes them more intimidating than effective. Excessive barking can be a problem. They are not very sociable with strangers, and moderately sociable with children. They do like to play, however, and can make an excellent and lively playmate for a gentle child. They may be scrappy with strange dogs, but most can live peacefully with other dogs and pets in the household as long as there is a clear dominance hierarchy.

Min Pins love to play, and provide their families with hours of entertainment. One need only watch a Min Pin of any age at play with its cache of toys to realize that perhaps the real reason it has been nicknamed the "king of toys" is that surely no dog enjoys toys as much as a Min Pin!

In a survey of miniature pinscher owners, barking, running away, dominance struggles, guarding of food or objects from family members, and snapping were considered the most common behavior problems. Some breeders do not advise first-time dog owners to get a Min Pin. Others advocate that Min Pins can make an excellent pet even for a first-time dog owner as long as you take the time to train and socialize your dog, and are educated about the idiosyncrasies of this cocky little dog.

Who should not have a Min Pin? If a primary requirement of your prospective dog is that it be a jogging companion (unless you plan very short jogs), protection dog, constant cuddler, fawning admirer, or snap-to-it Lassie clone, you may wish to explore some other breeds in comparison to the Min Pin. If your household is made up of a throng of unruly children or large dogs, ask yourself if a small dog would be safe from accidents. If the Min Pin looks like a prospective moneymaker, read the chapter on breeding (see page 67) and then see if you still think the Min Pin is your ticket to a life of leisure.

Then who would want a Min Pin? Ideal Min Pin owners are patient, gentle, and firm, and with a very good sense of humor. They want a lively dog that will enliven their lives. They don't want a dog as an inanimate ornament, or an automated robot; they want a quick-witted, free-spirited, graceful clown with which they can truly share their lives on a nearly equal partnership, rather than master-servant, basis.

Many breeds can be described as "acting sort of like a such and such"; the Min Pin is one-of-a-kind. Their owners like it that way. Make every effort to get to know some Min Pins at home; you may very well decide that a Min Pin is what your home is lacking.

The consummate watch dog, Min Pins never miss a thing.

Upkeep

The miniature pinscher is in many ways the toy dog for people who don't usually care for toy dogs. There is nothing "sissy" about this breed, either in appearance, demeanor, or hardiness. Still, no matter how big these dogs consider themselves, they are little dogs and can get hurt by big things. The Min Pin's small bones are extremely dense and strong for their size, but they still are relatively delicate. Added to the reckless devil-may-care personality so very typical of the Min Pin, and the only wonder is that more broken bones are not seen. They are not the breed for a household full of rambunctious children or careless adults. A minor accident for a large dog could prove to be a major accident for a dog this size. An attack from a large dog could prove fatal, so the Min Pin must always be watched when outside of a fenced area, especially because it is likely to be the one that initiates a fracas!

There are many advantages to being small. A small food bill is one of them. Almost everything costs less for small dogs, including boarding, bathing, shipping, housing, and even clothing. Best of all, they fit in your sports car, your apartment, your bed, and your lap!

The Min Pin is a fastidiously clean breed, with little doggy odor. It seldom requires bathing, and only needs a weekly brushing. Its small size and short coat make shedding a minimal problem.

Min Pins demand a soft bed and many creature comforts. They do not like cold weather and cannot be expected to live outdoors. Although of an independent nature, these dogs will not be happy removed from the hustle and bustle of your family life.

The Min Pin loves to move! It requires plenty of exercise but is capable of getting it in a small area, even if it's in your living room when you are trying to concentrate on other matters. Although not physically suited to marathon running, it will happily join you for a short jog, a game of fetch, or a roundup of unsuspecting squirrels. Min Pins must be provided with toys lest their boundless energy lead them into mischief.

Health and Longevity

Any dog that moves as much as a Min Pin had better be healthy. In fact, Min Pins are an extremely hardy breed, with no particularly prevalent health problems. They commonly live to be about 12 years of age, with many individuals enjoying life well into their teens. Although they do slow considerably with time, they typically enjoy good health even into old age.

Purebred dogs are often beset by hereditary health problems that are more prevalent in particular breeds. The most well documented of these problems are those involving joints and eyes.

In Min Pins the most common skeletal ailment is Legg-Perthes (or Calve-Perthes) disease (aseptic femoral head necrosis), evidenced by limping in older puppies. Surgery or immobilization may be required. This is a relatively common problem of small breeds, and is in some ways the small breed analog of hip dysplasia, which is more common in large breeds. (Hip dysplasia has been reported in Min Pins, but is rare.) Both conditions affect the hip joint, but Legg-Perthes involves degeneration of the head of the femur bone, and usually affects only one leg. Preliminary data indicate that Legg-Perthes disease may be recessively inherited; hip dysplasia involves the interplay of many genes with environmental factors.

Another common problem of small breeds is patellar luxation, where the kneecap does not properly fit into the groove that should hold it into place. As a result, it sometimes pops out of place, causing the dog to hold its leg up until it pops back in. This, too, is seen in Min Pins, but not with the frequency as in some other small breeds.

A common visual problem in many breeds is progressive retinal atrophy (PRA); it, too, has been reported in the Min Pin, but is not common. PRA begins as night blindness in the adult dog, gradually resulting in total blindness. Veterinary ophthalmologists can diagnose the disorder in young puppies before any problems would be noticed by the owner. The condition is inherited as a simple recessive trait.

Inguinal hernias are not uncommon. Although they are thought to have a hereditary component, the mode of transmission is complex and not understood at present.

The breed is prone to a variety of skin problems, including demodectic mange, but perhaps no more than any other breed. Skin problems are in general the number one complaint of all dog breeds treated by veterinarians. The "blues" have a decided tendency to have hair loss problems.

Some new owners may not realize that the distinctive ear shape of the Min Pin is not natural, but results from cropping the ears at about three months of age. Prospective owners who oppose cropping should make sure they like the appearance of an uncropped Min Pin. Cropping does add some expense, and entails postoperative pain for the pup, as well as additional care from the owner for about one month. Tails are usually docked at birth.

Min Pin Preferences

It takes a special person to choose a special dog. Congratulations on choosing one of the most special of breeds, the miniature pinscher. But your decisions are far from over. You will want to get the most special of miniature pinschers, a dog that will be a part of your family and life for the next 10 to 15 years. Spend the time now to make those years the best possible.

Puppy or Adult?

Although most prospective owners think in terms of getting a puppy, don't dismiss the idea of acquiring an older Min Pin. No one can deny that a puppy is cute and fun, but a puppy is much like a baby; you can't ever be too busy to walk, feed, supervise, or clean. If you work or have limited patience, consider an older puppy or adult because it won't require so much intensive care. Because Min Pin adults are so puppyish, they may just combine the best of both worlds.

An adult may arrive with a host of bad habits, however; if raised in a kennel, an older dog may have a difficult time adjusting to family life or children. Even for a family-oriented dog the transition period may be difficult, as Min Pins tend to become very attached to one person and do not warm immediately to new people. With patience and time, you will become that one person; such dogs often tend to ultimately become even more deeply attached to their new owners.

Most puppies are ideally brought home between 8 and 12 weeks of age, but if you definitely want a show-quality dog you may have to wait until the pups are much older. Some concessions may have to be made to accommodate ear cropping. No matter what the age, if the puppy has been properly socialized, your Min Pin will soon blend into your family life and love you as though it's always owned you.

Male or Female?

The choice of male versus female is largely one of personal preference, but keep the following pros and cons in mind.

A stag red can't resist a chance to play.

Males are the cockier of this already cocky breed. Unless neutered, they tend to become preoccupied with flirting with the females and sparring with the males. Some may also lift their legs in the house. At the same time,

The subtle hues of a blue miniature pinscher, although not admissible under the AKC standard, are nonetheless undeniably elegant.

many breeders contend that males are actually sweeter and tend to be more affectionate than females.

Females are slightly smaller, but no less feisty, than males. They come in estrus ("season" or "heat") twice a year; this lasts for three weeks, during which time you must keep her away from amorous neighborhood males that have chosen your house as the place to be. You must also contend with her bloody discharge during her season, but luckily it is slight in most Min Pins.

Most of the problems associated with either sex can be overcome by neutering. And if the prospects of making more money by breeding a Min Pin of one sex as opposed to the other enter into your decision, you should reconsider getting a dog at all. You're buying a family member, not livestock; besides, if you depend on the money you could make from breeding Min Pins, then welcome to the poorhouse!

Color Choices

The most popular colors are the reds, either a deep rich mahogany "stag red" (which are often born almost black, and gradually lose most of the black hairs with maturity), or a bright clear red (which may be an even lighter red as a puppy). Black and rust Min Pins have the same basic color pattern that is seen on Doberman pinschers or Manchester terriers. Less common are the chocolate Min Pins, with the same markings as the black and rust but in a dilute brown tone. These dogs usually have amber-colored eyes and brown noses. The genetics of these coat colors are outlined in the breeding chapter. There are also "blue" Min Pins, which is a light gray version of the black and rust. These dogs are not allowed to be shown. Rarely, fawn Min Pins occur, but these, too, are not showable. The blues and fawns tend to have some hair and skin problems.

In all colors, the presence of white spots over 0.5 inch (1.3 cm) in diameter or a patch of black hair surrounded by rust ("thumb marks") on the front of either front ankle is not acceptable for show potential Min Pins.

All Min Pins Are Not Created Equal

Although at first glance most Min Pins may look alike, to the experienced eye there are dramatic differences between individuals. The standard of perfection for the breed does not cover every detail and is open to interpretation in several areas. Not all breeders agree on just how refined a Min Pin should be, or just how high they should prance, or any of a number of other variable traits. No dog is perfect, so some breeders may emphasize perfect showmanship, whereas others perfect proportions, and others perfect movement. As you see more Min Pins from different lineages, these differences will become more apparent to you, and you may begin to form an opinion as to which traits are most important to you. The more subtle differences will probably matter to you only if you wish to acquire a show- or breeding-quality dog.

Dogs can be graded as pet, show, and breeding quality. Pet-quality dogs have one or more traits that would make winning with them in the show ring difficult to impossible. A common reason in males is the failure of one or both testicles to descend into the scrotum. Such dogs can be gorgeous breed representatives, but cannot be shown. However, most veterinarians suggest the retained testicle be removed as it is more cancer prone, so this is an added expense you must anticipate. Another reason might be any of several small flaws that would never be evident to any but the most ardent Min Pin fancier:

The uncropped Min Pin has a special appeal and many people feel they have more expressive ears, as they may stand at attention when alert, flop over when at ease, or even have one of each!

flaws such as a missing tooth, a long back, or straight shoulder angles. These dogs, too, make beautiful pets. Somewhat questionable are those with flaws that make them non-Min Pin-like

After cropping, ears must be trained to stand. One way is by delicately taping them to a cap made of an inverted cup. Pups should be especially coddled during this time.

13

(remember, you want a Min Pin in part because you like how they look, right?). Such a flaw might be a rounded Chihuahua-like head, bulgy eyes, floppy ears, lack of hackney movement, or oversize. Finally, there are flaws that make pet quality not even pet quality: flaws in temperament such as shyness or aggressiveness, or in health. Being a pet is the most important role a dog can fulfill.

Show-quality dogs should first of all be pet quality; that is, they should have good temperament and health. On top of this, they should be able to compete in the show ring with a reasonable expectation of finishing a championship. Showing a dog can open an entire new world of exciting wins, crushing losses, eccentric friends, travel to exotic fairgrounds in remote cities, and endless opportunities to spend money. It is inexplicably addicting. You should attend several shows before deciding you want to be a participant. Your search for a show-quality dog will require considerable effort on your part. Begin by seeing as many Min Pins in action (at dog shows or breeders' homes) and in print (books and magazines) as possible. Ask breeders what they consider to be the good and bad points of their stock. Be forewarned: it will be a rare day when two breeders agree on what is the most perfect Min Pin, so in the end it will be up to you alone to make an informed choice based upon your own sense of Min Pin perfection.

With few exceptions, breeding-quality dogs come from impeccable backgrounds, and are of even higher show quality than are show-quality dogs. Breeding quality means more than the ability to impregnate or conceive, but far too often these are the only criteria applied to prospective parents by owners unduly impressed by an AKC registration certificate. It is

Cropping ears involves surgically removing the outer edge of the ear, resulting in a narrower, more tapered shape. Not all uncropped ears will stand erect.

difficult to pick a show-quality puppy at an early age; it is impossible to pick a breeding-quality puppy.

Those Irresistible Ears

Part of the appeal of the miniature pinscher is its alert, intelligent expression, which is in part due to its characteristic cropped ears. Cropping is not mandated for show-quality Min Pins, but most show dogs do have cropped ears and although it shouldn't matter in judging, there is a perception that uncropped dogs are at a disadvantage in the show ring. Uncropped ears give the dog a softer, less keen expression. They are longer, more rounded, and especially wider at the base. Many times they will not stand up, so that cropping is necessary to avoid a flop ear. Hanging ears do not predispose the dog to ear problems, as is sometimes argued. There are breeders specializing in freestanding uncropped ears, however, and most uncropped ears can be encouraged to stand by taping them during critical growth phases.

Cropping requires surgery under general anesthesia at about 12 weeks of age. It involves cutting away the outer section of the ear from top to bottom, suturing the cut surface, adhering the ears to a little "dunce cap" for two to three weeks postoperatively, and then taping them for support for some time longer (varying with individuals). The procedure is somewhat painful for the puppy and if you are definitely not interested in showing, you may not wish to subject your new dog and yourself to this process. Some people consider cropping cruel and it is against the law in some countries. Some veterinarians are choosing not to crop ears for humane reasons. Speak to your dog's breeder about your desires, and make sure you are in agreement before you buy a puppy.

In Search of the Perfect Min Pin

Whether you want pet, show, or breeding quality, you must be very careful about where you find your Min Pin. You want to avoid puppies from parents whose only claim to breeding quality is fertility. And you want to avoid buying from a breeder whose only claim to that title is owning a fertile Min Pin.

You may think that if you only want pet quality you don't have to be so careful. But consider again the most important attributes of a pet: good health and good temperament. Many people mistakenly believe that the phrase "AKC registered" is an assurance of quality. But it can no more assure quality any more than the registration of your car is an assurance of automotive quality. Few people would buy a car from a stranger without extensive checking and testing, but many people answer the first ad they see in the paper and come home with a Min Pin puppy about which they know nothing except that it is AKC registered.

Buy the best dog, with the best parents, from the best breeder, possible. It is best if you can actually see the parents and the puppies, and if you get some type of guarantee. But a word of caution about guarantees from any source: no guarantee can reimburse you for your broken heart when your puppy dies. And replacement guarantees that require you to return the original dog aren't worth much when you already love that original dog.

Common Sources

Some pros and cons of the more common sources for acquiring a miniature pinscher follow.

Pet stores: Pet stores are a traditional source of puppies in our society, and are often the only place that the average person thinks of when it comes to buying a puppy. Most pet stores can obtain any breed of dog within a short period of time. But they do this by obtaining puppies from large breeding operations, where puppies have little opportunities for socialization and parents are usually of poor quality and often poor health. Because pet stores have many expenses to meet, puppies tend to be rather costly compared to some other sources. Better pet stores will carefully screen their sources, hire workers to play with and exercise puppies, and provide a health guarantee. Like all of the sources listed here, pet stores vary in the quality of knowledge and stock available. One Min Pin buyer was told by a pet store worker that the reason the Min Pin in the window was so expensive was that it was top show and breeding quality. The prospective buyer was astute enough to notice that it could qualify as neither, because it was a male with both testicles undescended!

Pet stores are an excellent source for high-quality dog food, collars, leashes, toys, and many wonderful accessories, but are not the optimal source for a new family member unless time is the primary consideration, which it should never be!

Newspaper advertisements: You may find an ad for a miniature pinscher in the newspaper. Some ads are placed by reputable breeders and could be a good source of a wonderful pet. But most are not. Still, they may be worth a call. A good sign is an ad that mentions titled parents, which would be an indication that the breeder is concerned with quality. A statement that the pups are not yet available indicates that the breeder is not trying to simply "move" them at a premature age. A mention that pups are raised in the home reveals attention to socialization. Although you cannot expect a health guarantee to cover everything, the promise of one shows the breeder is confident in the health of the puppies and will stand behind them after the sale. A mention that breed information is available, and a willingness to discuss pros and cons of the breed, is a very good sign.

Stay away from ads that refer to the breed as miniature Dobermans, or as thoroughbreds, or full blooded, or papered, all of which are not terms a knowledgeable breeder would use. Don't be impressed by the promise of many champions in the pedigree. In any pedigree you will find many champions. A typical pedigree includes over sixty dogs; the law of averages states that several of these would probably be champions, and if these champions are more than two generations back their effect upon these puppies is minimal. Nor should you be impressed by the statement that the pups have been vaccinated and wormed. All puppies should be vaccinated and wormed by selling age, so if the breeder considers this a big deal, these pups probably don't have a lot going for them.

Ask questions such as "Why did you breed the litter?" "How did you choose the sire?" If they answer that they bred the litter because the dam is a good representative of her breed (although not perfect), and they thought she could produce a quality litter if bred correctly, keep listening. If they chose the sire because he was recommended by a breeder as a good complement to their bitch, although a long distance away, put this person on your list of possibles. But if they answer that they bred the litter because "Min Pins are fine little moneymakers" or "Sparky here has got a pedigree as long as your arm, and Min Pins are a rare breed, and although she's never been to a show we were told she's the best one this side of the Ozarks," or that they chose the stud because "He's the biggest Min Pin around, and besides, he lives right down the street," then decline. Do not even look at the puppies lest you get caught up in their undeniable cuteness (*any* Min Pin puppy is cute, no matter how poorly bred).

Dog magazines: A quick way to contact several serious breeders is to look in the classified section of one of the monthly dog magazines available at larger newsstands. For show quality, try *TNT Toys* magazine. The disadvantage is that if the breeder is located a distance from you then you will not be able to evaluate their dogs in the flesh, and you will not be able to choose your own puppy. Also, shipping adds an additional expense and can be stressful for an older puppy.

Dog shows: If at all possible attend a dog show. You can contact the AKC for dates of shows in your area; these are also listed in *Dog World* magazine. Most shows start at 8 A.M. so, unless you know when the miniature pinschers are being judged, you must get there early or risk missing them altogether. Tell the Min Pin exhibitors of your interest and arrange to talk with several after they have finished in the show ring. Some dogs may be shown by professional dog handlers;

these are the jockeys of the dog show world. Talk to them, too, because they will be able to give you a more unbiased view of the Min Pin in comparison to the other breeds they show. Incidentally, don't be swayed by who wins or loses on that one day. It's *your* opinion that matters, not that of one judge.

Why contact a show breeder if all you want is a pet? Because these breeders will have raised your pet as though it were their next Best in Show winner. It will have received the same prenatal care, nutrition, and socialization as every prospective show dog in that litter. And the breeder should be knowledgeable and conscientious enough to have also considered temperament and health when planning the breeding. If this is to be your first Min Pin, then you will need continued advice from an experienced Min Pin owner as your puppy grows. The serious hobby breeder is just a phone call away, and will be concerned that both you and the puppy are getting along well. In fact, because many breeders will expect to keep in touch with the owners of all of the puppies, whether pet or show, throughout their lives, you may find yourself a member of an adopted extended family of sorts, all of whom are available for advice, help, consolation, and celebration. Breeders who belong to some breed clubs must adhere to the club code of ethics. Finally, because in some sense the non-show puppy is a by-product of the litter, these breeders are not out to make a buck from these puppies, and prices are generally quite reasonable.

Breed clubs and rescue organizations: The Miniature Pinscher Club of America, Inc. (see Useful Addresses and Literature, page 86) is an excellent source of reputable breeders. In addition, if you are interested in an older dog, ask to be put in contact with the breed rescue group, which finds homes for Min Pins that have fallen upon hard times.

Animal shelters: As the Min Pin's popularity continues to grow, more Min Pins are finding their way into homes not suited for their temperaments, and may eventually be given up for adoption. If you do find a Min Pin in a shelter, ascertain why it was surrendered by its former family. Was its typical Min Pin lifestyle incompatible with theirs, or did this particular Min Pin have insurmountable behavioral problems? Does it have behavioral problems brought about by living with a family that could not cope with the Min Pin persona? If so, speak with a veterinarian, knowledgeable dog trainer, or behaviorist and ask what the treatment and prognosis is for that behavior. Although adopting a dog often means a lot of work, there is immense satisfaction in knowing that you are that dog's savior, and are offering it a life filled with love and understanding that it may never have experienced before.

Though still too young to go to their new homes, these pups may be impossible to choose between. If you have no other pets and are away a lot, consider saying, "I'll take both!"

Narrowing the Field

Tell the breeder exactly what qualities you want in a Min Pin, if you have a sex, color, or age preference, and whether you want pet or show quality. It is not fair to you or the breeder to ask for a show puppy you never intend to show, and it is equally unfair to both of you to get a pet puppy and then try to show it. Many, many hard feelings have arisen because of this seemingly small oversight. A good breeder should in turn ask you about your previous history with dogs, why you want a Min Pin, what you know about living with a Min Pin, and what living arrangements you have planned for the dog.

Ask about the parents. Do they have conformation or obedience titles? This is not only important if you want a show/obedience prospect, but again can give you a clue about the care taken with the litter. What kind of temperaments do the parents and the puppies have? If some puppies are being sold as pet quality, why? Have the parents or puppies had any health problems? Have the parents been screened for hip or eye problems? If the breeder states that the parents have an Orthopedic Foundation for Animals (OFA) hip clearance or Canine Eye Registration Foundation (CERF) eye clearance number, then this is an excellent sign. However, don't write a Min Pin breeder off your list if their stock has not been checked, because the problems are not widespread in the breed. But do proceed with extreme caution if the breeder's reply to your inquiry is any of the following: 1) "Min Pins have *no* problems," 2) "My lines have never had a single hereditary problem," or 3) "Huh?"

Ask the breeder about the terms of sale. Don't fall in love with a puppy and then have to walk away because an agreement could not be reached. There are several possibilities, the easiest being that you will pay a set amount (usually cash) and receive full ownership. If registration papers cost extra, shy away. Puppy and papers should always be a package deal. Sometimes breeders will insist upon having a pet puppy neutered before supplying the papers, or they may stipulate that a pet puppy is to have a "limited registration," which means it cannot be shown or bred. These arrangements are acceptable but should be in writing. If you are making installment payments, the breeder will probably retain the papers or a co-ownership until the last installment. Sometimes a breeder will insist upon co-owning the puppy permanently. If any co-ownership involves future breeding of the puppy (especially a female) and "puppy-back" agreements, you probably should again shy away. Such arrangements invariably lead to problems. If the co-ownership is for insurance that the dog will be returned to the breeder in the event you cannot keep it, then such an agreement is probably acceptable. Any such terms should be in writing.

To Pick a Min Pin Puppy

Once you have narrowed down your list, if possible, arrange to visit the breeder. Most modern "kennels" are a collection of only a few dogs that are first of all the breeder's pets. However large or small the operation, look for facilities that are clean and safe. Again, these are clues about the care given your prospective puppy. The adults should be clean, groomed, and in apparent good health. They should neither try to attack you nor cower from you. Look to the adults for the dog your puppy will become. If you don't care for their looks or temperaments, say good-bye.

If you are considering more than one breeder, be honest about it. Breeders talk to each other and will find out you are comparison shopping anyway. Always go to view the puppies prepared to leave without one if you don't see exactly what you want. Remember, no good breeder wants you to take a puppy you are not 110 percent crazy about. This is not something you can trade in once you find what you really want. Don't lead the breeder on if you have decided against a purchase; he may have another buyer in line. Finally, don't visit from one breeder to another on the same day, and certainly do not visit the animal shelter beforehand. Puppies are vulnerable to many deadly diseases that you can transmit by way of your hands, clothes, and shoes. How tragic it would be if the breeder's invitation for you to view their babies ended up killing them.

These puppies are fragile little beings, and you must be extremely careful where you step and how you handle them. If you have children with you, don't allow them to run around or play with the puppies unsupervised. In addition, your entire family should know how to properly hold a puppy. Never pick up a puppy by its legs or head or tail; cradle the puppy with both hands, one under the chest, the other under the hindquarters, and with the side of the pup secure against your chest. Keep a firm hold lest the pup try to jump out of your arms unexpectedly. Even at a young age mistreatment or negligence might have damaged your puppy's temperament or health, so watch the breeder to see that he or she treats the pups with love and gentleness.

As you finally look upon this family of canine jumping beans, you may suddenly find it very difficult to be objective. How will you ever decide? If you want a show puppy, let the breeder decide. In fact, the breeder knows the puppies' personalities better than you will in the short time you can evaluate

them, so listen carefully to any suggestions the breeder has even for a pet. It is human nature to pick "extremes," but most breeders would advise against choosing either the boldest Min Pin puppy or any pup that acts shy. But first decide if this is the litter for you.

By eight weeks of age, baby Min Pins should look like miniature adults. Of course, they will look comparatively stockier and uncoordinated, and their ears may not yet be fully erect, but they should generally be recognizable as miniature pinschers. Dark nose pigmentation, absent at birth, should be present by this age. The tail should be docked, and usually the dewclaws. The ears will not be cropped until 12 weeks of age. Ears that are not standing by 12 weeks of age will probably never stand unless they are cropped. In an unpublished study of 50 Min Pin puppies, those that were between 6¼" to 8" at age 8 weeks, or 7½" to 9½" at 12 weeks, grew to be of proper height as adults. Note that all measurements

Hold a puppy firmly and securely so that it can not be dropped or unexpectedly squirm out of your arms.

are made of height at withers. Normal Min Pin puppies are friendly, curious, and attentive. If they are apathetic or sleeping, it could be because they have just eaten, but it could also be because they are sickly.

The puppies should be clean, with no missing hair, crusted or reddened skin, or signs of parasites. Eyes, ears, and nose should be free of discharge. Examine the eyelids if such a discharge is present to ensure that it is not due to the lids or lashes rolling in on the eye and causing irritation. The teeth should be straight and meet up evenly, with the top incisors just overlapping the lower incisors. The gums should be pink; pale gums may indicate anemia. The area around the anus should have no hint of irritation or recent diarrhea. Puppies should not be thin or excessively potbellied. The belly should have no large bumps indicating a hernia. By the age of 12 weeks, male puppies should have both testicles descended in the scrotum. If the

puppy of your choice is limping, or exhibits any of the above traits, express your concern and ask to either come back next week to see if it has improved, or to have your veterinarian examine it. In fact, any puppy you buy should be done so with the stipulation that it is pending a health check (at your expense) by your veterinarian.

The breeder should furnish you with a complete medical history including dates of vaccinations and worming. If the puppies ears have not been cropped, discuss the pros and cons of this procedure with the breeder before leaving with your puppy. Veterinarians differ in their cropping skill, and your breeder may wish to suggest a veterinarian with Min Pin cropping expertise. If the ears have already been cropped, be sure you understand any special care you must give them.

You may still find it nearly impossible to decide which whirling dervish will be yours. Don't worry: no matter which one you choose, it will be the best one. In years to come, you will wonder how you were so lucky to have picked the marvel Min Pin of the millennium; you must realize that your Min Pin will be wonderful in part because you are going to make it that way!

What's in a Name?

Be sure to ask the breeder what name your puppy knows. Most breeders call all of their puppies by some generic name, such as "pup." Just continue to call yours by the same name until you have something better picked out. Your pup will learn a new name quickly at this age, especially if it means food or fun is on the way. Be careful about the name you choose; for example, "Napoleon" starts with a sound that is too similar to "No"; the same is true for "Nomad," which also sounds like "bad." Test your chosen name to be sure that it does not sound like a reprimand or command.

A healthy 8-week-old with good conformation.

You should not leave with your puppy without the blue AKC registration application signed by both you and the breeder. This is an extremely valuable document; do not misplace it or forget to send it in! Ask the breeder if there are any requirements concerning the puppy's registered name; most show breeders will want the first name to be their kennel name. You should also have received a pedigree with your puppy; if not, you can buy a copy of its pedigree from the AKC when you send in the registration papers.

Min Pin Mine

Congratulations on your new family member! The effort you've put into your choice will pay off in the years to come. Remember, it costs as much in both time and money to raise a poor Min Pin as it does a good one—and sometimes more!

You have a lifetime of experiences to share with your new Min Pin. The remainder of your little dog's life will be spent under your care and guidance. Both of you will change through the years. Accept that your Min Pin will change as it matures: from the cute, (somewhat) eager to please, baby, to the cute, mischievous, often disobedient adolescent, then to the self-reliant (but sometimes disobedient) adult partner, and finally the proud but frail senior (occasionally disobedient just for old time's sake). Be sure that you remember the promise you made to yourself and your future puppy before you made the commitment to share your life: to keep your interest in your dog and care for it everyday of its life with as much love and enthusiasm as you did the first day it arrived home. Your life may change dramatically in the years to come: divorce, new baby, new home—for better or worse, your Min Pin will still depend on you and still love you, and you need to remain as loyal to your Min Pin as your Min Pin will be to you.

Raising Your Miniature Pinscher

Not So Fast...

After you have selected your Min Pin-to-be, it's only natural to want to bring it home right away. But take a minute to look around your house. Is it really ready to accept a ricocheting Min Pin bullet? It will be a lot easier to get it into Min Pin-proof shape now than it will be when you have a little puppy undoing everything just as fast as you can do it! So channel your excitement and make sure everything is just perfect and waiting for the new addition.

If you are contemplating bringing your pup home as a Christmas pre-sent, you should think again. The heartwarming scene you may have imagined of the children discovering the baby asleep among the other gifts beneath the tree on Christmas morning is not realistic. The real scene is more often that of a crying, confused baby who may have vented its anxiety on the other gifts and left you some additional "gifts" of its own! Don't bring a new puppy into the hectic chaos of Christmas morning. Not only does this add to what is bound to be a very confusing and intimidating transition for your Min Pin, but a puppy should not be expected to compete with all of the toys and games that children may be receiving. Every pup needs the undivided attention of its new family at this crucial time in its life. Instead, a photograph or videotape of your special Min Pin-to-be will have to suffice until some of the holiday madness has subsided. But you can start buying Min Pin paraphernalia right away!

For shop-aholics, here's your big chance. Visit a large pet store, or a dog show, or peruse a discount pet catalog, and get shopping. It's not really true that "all you add is love" (but you'll need lots of that, too)!

The Min Pin Den

Many new dog owners are initially appalled at the idea of putting their pet in a cage as though it were some wild beast. At times, though, your Min Pin pup can be a wild beast, and a cage is one way to save your home from ruination and yourself from insanity.

An X-pen provides an indoor yard and is perfect if you must be gone for long periods.

The Homecoming Kit

• Buckle collar (cat collar for puppies): for wearing around the house.
• Nylon or fine chain choke collar: safer for walking on-lead.
• Lightweight leash: nylon, web, or leather—never chain! An adjustable show lead is good for puppies.
• Lightweight retractable leash: better for older dogs; be sure not to drop them, as they retract toward the pup and can frighten them.
• Stainless steel flat-bottomed food and water bowls: avoid plastic; it can cause allergic reactions and hold germs.
• Cage: just large enough for an adult to stand up in without having to lower its head.
• Exercise pen: tall enough that an adult can't jump over, or preferably with a top.
• Toys: latex squeakies, fleece-type toys, balls, stuffed animals, stuffed socks. Make sure squeakies and the eyes of stuffed animals can't be ingested.
• Chew bones: the equivalent of a teething ring for babies.
• Anti-chew preparations.
• Baby gate(s): better than a shut door for placing parts of your home off-limits.
• Soft brush.
• Nail clippers.
• Dog shampoo.
• First aid kit.
• Sweater: for cold climates.
• Food: start with the same food the pup is currently eating.
• Dog bed: a round fleece-lined cat bed is heavenly, but you can also use the bottom of a plastic cage, or any cozy box, padding with two layers of blankets to accommodate a burrowing Min Pin. Wicker will most likely be chewed to shreds, and should be avoided!
• Camera and film! (a telephoto lens is a necessity.)

Make sure that toys or any parts thereof cannot be ingested.

But a cage can also provide a quiet haven for your Min Pin. Just as you hopefully find peace and security as you sink into your own bed at night, your pup needs a place that it can call its own, a place it can seek out whenever the need for rest and solitude arises. Used properly, your Min Pin will come to think of its cage not as a way to keep itself in, but as a way to keep others out! Like its wild ancestors, the Min Pin appreciates the security of its own den.

A cage is the canine equivalent of an infant's crib. It is a place for naptime, a place where you can leave your pup without worry of it hurting itself or your home. It is not a place for punishment, nor is it a storage box for your dog when you're through playing with it. Place the cage in a corner of a quiet room, but not too far from the rest of the family. Place the pup in the cage when it begins to fall asleep, and it will become accustomed to using it as its bed. Be sure to place a soft double pad in the bottom. And by taking the pup directly from the cage to the outdoors upon awakening, the cage will be one of the handiest housebreaking aids at your disposal.

The Min Pin Pen

An exercise pen (commonly referred to as an "X-pen") also fulfills many of the same functions as a cage. These are transportable wire folding "playpens" for dogs, typically about 4 by 4 feet (1.2 × 1.2 m). In fact, if you must be gone for hours at a time, they are the perfect answer because the pup can relieve itself on paper in one corner, sleep on a soft bed in the other, and frolic with its toys all over!

Chew bones are the equivalent of a teething ring for babies.

The traditional wicker basket is short-lived around young Min Pins.

It's like having a little yard inside; actually, it's the canine equivalent of the baby's playpen.

Decide now where you intend to keep your new family member. Min Pins are obviously *not* outdoor dogs, although they will enjoy the opportunity to spend part of their days outside, weather permitting. Your Min Pin will want to be in the thick of things,

These dogs are drawn to cozy beds and warm sunbeams. Don't be surprised to find one burrowed under your covers!

and participate in everything your family does. So plan for your Min Pin to be quartered in the house where it can be around activity, but not necessarily always underfoot.

It is best that the new puppy not have the run of the entire house. Choose an easily Min Pin-proofed room where you spend a lot of time, preferably one that is close to a door leading outside. Kitchens and dens are usually ideal. When you must leave your dog for some time, you may wish to place it in a cage, X-pen, secure room, or outdoor kennel. Bathrooms have the disadvantage of being so confining and isolated that puppies may become destructive; garages have the disadvantage of also housing many poisonous items.

Min Pin Mishap Prevention

Outside

If you have a yard, the number one safety item is a secure fence. Min Pins, like all dogs, would love to run loose and rule the neighborhood. But they probably wouldn't live long if they did. Because Min Pins are blissfully ignorant of the dangers that lurk for a little dog in the big outdoors, it is vital that you prevent such roaming. Luckily, Min Pins are not known for their fence jumping prowess (although they can jump considerably higher than most other dogs their size), but they are adept burrowers and squeezers. A small hole in the fence is all one needs to wriggle its way to freedom. Many dogs are actually inadvertently taught to escape by their owners. Perhaps the new owner has an old fence, and decides to wait and see if it will hold the dog. When the dog squeezes out of the biggest holes, the owner patches those. Then the dog looks for the next biggest hole, and squeezes out of it. Finally, as the fence comes to resemble a patchwork quilt, the dog is squeezing through holes that you would swear couldn't possibly accommodate a dog with bones. Yet had the fence only had such tiny holes in the first place, the dog would never have learned to go through them. If you wanted your Min Pin to learn to squeeze through small passages, wouldn't you do so a little at a time? Then why use the same tactic to teach your dog *not* to squeeze through? If you want your dog to stay in the yard, make the yard Min Pin-proof from the very beginning.

Your fence must not only be strong enough to keep your dog in, but to keep stray dogs out. This is why the "invisible fences" that keep your dog within are no good for Min Pins. They don't keep other animals out. If you live in a rural area, wild animals (including alligators, coyotes, and hawks) may look upon your puppy as a snack. Still, the number one predator of any dog is the automobile. Good fences make live dogs!

There can still be dangers within the yard, though. Are there bushes with sharp, broken branches at Min Pin eye level? Are there trees with dead branches in danger of falling, or even heavy falling fruits or pinecones? Are there poisonous plants? (Some of the more deadly are yew, mistletoe, English holly berries, philodendron, Jerusalem cherry, azaleas, rhododendron, foxglove, water hemlock, milkweed, rattlebox, corn cockle, jimsonweed, jessamine, oleander, and castor bean). If you have a pool, be aware that although dogs are natural swimmers, a little Min Pin cannot pull itself up a swimming pool wall and can drown.

Finally, you must protect your Min Pin against unscrupulous humans, who may find an unchaperoned purebred to be an irresistible source of some imagined easy money. If you leave your Min Pin alone in your yard,

Min Pin poisons.

lock your gate, and take precautions to not make your defenseless friend a target for crime.

Inside
Min Pin-proofing your home has two goals: protecting your Min Pin, and protecting your home. The first step is to do everything you would do to baby-proof your home. Get down at puppy level and see what dangers beckon. Puppies love to chew electrical cords in half, and even lick outlets. These can result in severe burns, loss of the jaw and tongue, and death. Running into a sharp table corner could cause an eye injury. Jumping up on an unstable

Household Min Pin Killers
- Rodent baits
- Household cleaners
- Toilet fresheners
- Leaked antifreeze
- Drugs
- Some houseplants
- Chocolate (especially baker's chocolate)
- Nuts, bolts, and pennies
- Pins and needles
- Bones
- Loose toy parts

HOW-TO:
Understanding the Min Pin Mind

In order to share your life with your Min Pin, you need to realize that it inhabits a very different world than yours. The size difference is self-evident, but differences in the sensory worlds of humans and dogs are not as obvious.

Vision: The canine eye does not see the world with as much detail or color as does the human eye. Dogs can see colors, but their sense of color is like that of a color-blind person. That is, dogs confuse similar shades of yellow-green, yellow, orange, and red, but can see and discriminate blue, indigo, and violet from all other colors and each other as well as humans can. This does not mean the dog's eye is inferior to the human's; it is superior when it comes to seeing in very dim light.

Olfaction: The dog's sense of smell is renown, and even the Min Pin has olfactory abili-

Light passes through the cornea and pupil of the eye and is focused by the lens onto the retina. Min Pins are susceptible to disorders of both the lens and retina, which can impair vision.

Whether with cropped or uncropped ears, the Min Pin has acute hearing. Note that the deep canal makes the dog's ear susceptible to various fungal and bacterial infections.

ties that are beyond its owner's comprehension. It is as though humans are completely blind when it comes to the world of smell, and there is no way one can imagine the vastness of this sensory world that is so very apparent to your dog. The next time you become impatient when your dog wants to sniff something on a walk, consider it the same as when you stop to admire a sunset, much to your Min Pin's bewilderment.

Taste: Dogs also have a well-developed sense of taste, and have most of the same taste receptors that humans do. Research has shown that they prefer meat (not exactly earth-shaking news), and although there are many individual differences, the average dog prefers beef, pork, lamb, chicken, and horse meat, in that order.

Hearing: Dogs can hear much higher tones than can humans, and so can be irritated by high hums from your TV or from those ultrasonic flea collars. The Min Pin's prick ears are unencumbered by heavy fur and are ideally suited for

detecting and localizing sounds, more so than dogs with other ear configurations.

Pain: Many people erroneously believe that animals cannot feel pain, but common sense and scientific research indicate that dogs and other animals have a well-developed sense of pain. Many dogs are amazingly stoic, however, and their ability to deal with pain is not totally understood at present. Because a dog may not be able to express that it is in pain, you must be alert to changes in your dog's demeanor. A stiff gait, reluctance to get up, irritability, dilated pupils, whining, or limping are all indications that your dog is in pain.

Even the little miniature pinscher is a wolf at heart, and you can see it exhibit many of the same behavior patterns as its wild ancestors. Dogs, however, differ from wolves in being perpetual juveniles; they never mature mentally to the same level that wolves do. This is one of the results of domestication, and different breeds differ in the extent of this selected infantilism. Still, with careful observation, you can see the wolf in your house.

Extreme submission.

Let's play!

Wolves and dogs depend upon facial expressions and body language in social inter-actions:

• A yawn is often a sign of ner-vousness. Drooling can indicate extreme nervousness.

• A wagging tail, a lowered head, and exposed teeth upon greeting is a sign of submission.
• The combination of a lowered body, a wagging tail, lowered ears, urination, and perhaps even rolling over is a sign of extreme submission.
• The combination of exposed teeth, a high, rigidly held tail, raised hackles, very upright posture, a stiff-legged gait, a direct stare, forward pricked ears, and perhaps lifting its leg to mark a tree indicates very dominant, threatening behavior.
• The combination of a wag-ging tail, front legs and elbows on the ground and rear in the air, with or without vocaliza-

Aggression.

tions, is the classic "play-bow" position, and is an invitation for a game. This is the Min Pin's favorite pose!

object could cause it to come crashing down, perhaps crushing the puppy. Do not allow the puppy near the edges of high decks, balconies, or staircases.

Doors can be a hidden danger area. Everyone in your family must be made to understand the danger of slamming a door, which could catch a Min Pin and break a leg—or worse. Use doorstops to ensure that the wind does not blow doors suddenly shut, or that the puppy does not go behind the door to play. This can be a danger, because the gap on the hinged side of the door can catch and break a little Min Pin leg if the door is closed. Be especially cautious with swinging doors; a puppy may try to push one open, become caught, try to back out, and strangle. Clear glass doors may not be seen, and the puppy could be injured running into them. Never close a garage door with a Min Pin running about. Finally, doors leading to unfenced outdoor areas should be kept securely shut. A screen door is a vital safety feature; Min Pins are adept

With an eye out for potential adventure, the Min Pin is more than just another plaything with which to adorn your home. Without proper training, it will gladly take on the responsibility of home redecorator.

at streaking between your legs to freedom when you open the front door.

You've protected your Min Pin, now how about your home? Min Pins can make a mess far out of proportion to their size! Never leave your Min Pin puppy in a room in which there is something that if chewed into unrecognizable pieces, would upset you. Leather furniture is the world's biggest rawhide chewy to a puppy, and wicker can provide hours of chewing enjoyment. Puppies particularly like to chew items that carry your scent. Shoes, socks, eyeglasses, and clothing must be kept out of the youngster's reach. Remove anything breakable that you value from your Min Pin's reach. Remove books and papers. No need for a costly paper shredder when you have a Min Pin puppy! Move any houseplants that you would like to survive. The imagination of the Min Pin is never so obvious as when it is looking for trouble.

Your new white carpets (at least in the area between the cage and the door) can be covered with small washable rugs or indoor-outdoor carpeting until your puppy is housebroken. If you use an X-pen, cover the floor beneath it with thick plastic (an old shower curtain works well), and then add towels or washable rugs for traction and absorbency.

The Imminent Min Pin

Finally, it's homecoming time! If you work, try to bring the pup home on a weekend so that the first day with you won't be one spent alone. The ride home with you may be the puppy's first time in a car, and its first time away from the security of its home and former family. If possible, bring a family member to hold and comfort the puppy on the ride home. If it is a long ride, bring a cage. Be sure to take plenty of towels in case the puppy gets carsick. Never let a new puppy roam around the car, where it can cause, and have, accidents. Spend some time at the breeder's house while the puppy gets acquainted with you, and listen carefully to the breeder's instructions. Arrange for the puppy not to have eaten before leaving with you; this lessens the possibility of car sickness and helps the puppy learn that you will be its new provider when you get to its new home.

When you get home, put the puppy on-lead and carry it to the spot you have decided will be the elimination site. Puppies tend to relieve themselves in areas where they can smell that they have used before. This is why it is so critical to never let the pup have an accident indoors; if it does, clean and deodorize the spot thoroughly (using a non-ammonia based cleanser) and block the pup's access to that area. Once the puppy relieves itself, let it explore a little and then offer it a small meal. Now is not the time for all the neighbors to come visiting. You want your pup to know who its new family members will be, and more people will only add to the youngster's confusion. Nor is it the time for rough and tumble play, which could scare the puppy. Introductions to other family pets might also be better postponed.

Once the puppy has eaten, it will probably have to relieve itself again, so take it back out to the part of the yard you have designated as the elimination area. Remember to praise enthusiastically when the pup eliminates in the right place. When your Min Pin begins to act sleepy, place it in its cage so that it knows this is its special bed. A stuffed toy, hot water bottle, or ticking clock may help alleviate some of the anxiety of being left alone. You may wish to place the cage in your bedroom for this first night so that the puppy may be comforted by your pres-

With the affinity for climbing of a mountain goat, don't be surprised if your Min Pin claims the highest point available from which to survey its domain.

ence. Remember, this is the scariest thing that has ever happened in your puppy's short life; it has been uprooted from the security of a mother, littermates, and a loving breeder, so you must be comforting and reassuring on this crucial first night.

Min Pin Sin

Off-limits Training

You should have decided before your puppy came home what parts of your home will be off-limits. Make sure that every family member understands the rules, and that they understand that sneaking the puppy onto off-limit furniture, for example, is not doing the puppy any favor at all. Your puppy will naturally want to explore everywhere you let it, including climbing on furniture. A harsh "No!" and firm but gentle push away from the furniture should let it realize that this is neither acceptable nor rewarding behavior. Don't fling the pup off of furniture, or use mousetraps on furniture surfaces, because both practices are dangerous and absolutely a bad idea unless you like emergency visits to the veterinarian. There are several more humane items (available through pet catalogs) that emit a loud tone when a dog jumps on furniture, but these should not be necessary if you train your young puppy gently and consistently from the beginning.

Housebreaking

All canines have a natural desire to avoid soiling their denning area. As soon as young wolves are able to walk, they will teeter out of their den to relieve themselves away from their bedding. Because you are using a cage for your puppy's den, your Min Pin will naturally try to avoid soiling it. But puppies have very weak control over their bowels, so that if you don't take them to their elimination area often, they may not be able to avoid soiling. Further, if the cage is too large for the puppy, it may simply step away from the area it sleeps in and relieve itself at the other end of the cage. An overly large cage can be divided with a secure barrier until the puppy is larger or housebroken. Even so, just like the wolf cubs, your puppy may step just outside the door of the cage and eliminate there, because to the pup, that fulfills the natural requirement of not going in the den. The puppy has failed to realize that it has just soiled *your* den. And the more the pup soils in a particular spot, the more it is likely to return to that same spot.

To avoid accidents, learn to predict when your puppy will have to relieve itself. Immediately after awakening, and soon after heavy drinking or playing, your puppy will urinate. You will probably have to carry a younger puppy outside to get it to the elimination area on time. Right after eating, or if nervous, your puppy will have to defecate. Circling, whining, sniffing,

and generally acting worried usually signals that defecation is imminent. Even if the puppy starts to relieve itself, quickly but calmly scoop the pup up and carry it outside (the surprise of being picked up will usually cause the puppy to stop in midstream, so to speak). You can add a firm "No," but yelling and swatting are neither necessary nor effective. When the puppy does relieve itself at its outside elimination site, remember to heap on the praise and let your Min Pin puppy know how pleased you are.

If you cannot be with your puppy for an extended period, you may wish to leave it outside (weather permitting) so that it will not be forced to have an indoor accident. If this is not possible, you may have to paper train your puppy. Place newspapers on the far side of the room (or X-pen), away from the puppy's bed or water bowl; near a door to the outside is best. Place the puppy on the papers as soon as it starts to relieve itself. A convenient aspect of paper training is that the concept of using the paper will transfer to wherever you put the paper, so if you later take the paper outside, it can act as a training tool there. You can also litter box train your puppy. Place newspaper or even cat litter in a cat box; add some soiled newspaper or something with the scent of urine, and place the pup in the box when it begins to urinate. Apartment dwellers may find that a box-trained Min Pin is very convenient on rainy days.

No matter how wonderful and smart your Min Pin is, it probably will not have full control over its bowels until it is around six months of age. Meanwhile, set the stage for a perfect house pet, and chin up! It will get better!

How Many Min Pins?

There are certain advantages, and disadvantages, to having more than one dog. Two dogs are twice the fun of one, without being twice the work. Consider adding another pet if you are gone for most of the day. Min Pins generally get along well with each other and with other dogs and cats. However, two unneutered males, especially of the same age, are apt to engage in dominance disputes. On the other hand, intact males and females together will provide you with the biyearly problem of keeping Romeo and Juliet separated. Still, Min Pins can make close attachments with their housemates, and will enjoy hours of playing together. In fact, whereas in many ways two dogs are better than one, three dogs are also better than two! With two dogs, a problem can arise when one is left alone while you train or give personal attention to the other. With three, there is always a pair left.

When introducing new dogs, it is best if both are taken to a neutral site so that territoriality does not provoke aggression. Two people walking the dogs beside each other as they would on a regular walk is an ideal way for dogs to accept each other.

Young Min Pins are more likely to be hurt by a cat than the other way around. An older Min Pin can learn to like cats by introducing them gradually, inside of the house. The dog should be held on-leash initially, and the cat prevented from running, which would elicit a chase response in the dog. If the dog is fed every time the cat appears, it will come to really appreciate the cat. Many Min Pins have become fast friends with "their" pet cats.

Boarding

Sometimes you must leave your dog behind when you travel. Ask friends or your veterinarian for boarding kennel recommendations. The ideal kennel will be approved by the American Boarding Kennel Association (ABKA), have climate-controlled accommodations, and keep your Min Pin either indoors or in a combination indoor-outdoor run. Make an unannounced visit to the kennel and ask to see the facilities. Although you can't expect spotlessness and a perfumy atmosphere, most runs should be clean and the odor should not be overpowering. All dogs should have clean water and at least some dogs (including any Min Pins) should have bedding. Good kennels will require proof of immunizations, and an incoming check for fleas. They will allow you to bring toys and bedding, and will administer medication. Strange dogs should not be allowed to mingle, and the entire kennel area should be fenced.

Your dog may be more comfortable if an experienced pet sitter or responsible friend comes to your home and feeds and exercises your dog regularly. This works best if you have a doggy door. Don't forget your dog's

Teach children to respect and care for your new family member.

breeder. He or she may welcome a visit from the former puppy, and your Min Pin may feel more at home. But be sure that the facilities are safe and escape-proof in case your dog decides it wants to go home. Whatever means you choose, always leave emergency numbers and your veterinarian's name.

Missing Min Pin

If your little friend escapes or gets lost, you must act quickly in order to ensure its safe return. If your dog has recently escaped, don't wait for it to show up. Immediately go to the very worst place you could imagine it going. If you live near a highway, go there, and search backward toward your home. Be certain, however, that your dog does not find you first and follow you to the highway! And if you are driving, be certain that you do not drive recklessly and endanger your own dog's life should it return to you. If you still can't find your pet, get pictures of Min Pins and go door to door;

ask any workers or delivery persons in the area. Call the local animal control, police department, and veterinarians. If your dog is tattooed, contact the tattoo registry. Make up *large* posters with a picture of a Min Pin. Take out an ad in the local paper. Mention a reward, but do not specify an amount.

A word of caution: Never give anyone money before seeing your dog. There are a number of scams involving answering lost dog ads, many asking for money for shipping the dog back to you from a distance or for paying vet bills, when very often these people have not really found your dog. If your dog is tattooed, you can have the person read the tattoo to you in order to positively identify your pet. Other scammers actually steal your dog for reward money, and wait until you are desperate and will pay a high reward; and then have been known to also burglarize your home when you go to meet their partners to pick up the dog! The moral: protect your dog in the first place from theft or loss, and be wary when asked for money in return for your dog.

Even license tags cannot always ensure your dog's return, because these must be on the dog to be effective. Tattooing your Social Security number or your dog's registration number on the inside of its thigh provides a permanent means of identification; these numbers can be registered with one of the several lost pet recovery agencies. Microchip implants are painless, safe, permanent and can carry a lot of information, but should supplement other means of identification because not all shelters have chip scanners. You may wish to discuss this option with your veterinarian or local breeders.

Few things can surpass playing Min Pin pups for a display of nimbleness and agility, even at this young age.

Adventures with Min Pins

All work and no play would make owning a dog a very dull thing. But millions of people would not own dogs if that were *all* there was to it! For every moment of work, there are manyfold more moments of love and fun! Your Min Pin will demand that you take every opportunity to share an adventure, be it exploring the wilds of the great outdoors, or the folds of the blankets on your bed.

The Min Pin Afield

Min Pins can entertain themselves quite ably within the confines of your own yard, but they will jump at the chance to conquer new horizons. But take care that your Min Pin doesn't bite off more than it can chew. As big as it may think it is, the reality is that there are truly big dogs out there that may not fall for the Min Pin bluff. Keep an eye out for loose dogs, and snatch your little fellow up and out of reach at first sight. There are few places you can let your Min Pin loose without the danger of other loose, big dogs. Fenced ball fields or schoolyards may be safe, but always, always, clean up after your dog. It's a good idea to bring some treats so you can practice off-lead recalls. You may even want to make sure that your dog is already hungry (and maybe a little tired) before you go, if you have any doubts about its eager return.

Before walking on-lead, double-check that your dog's collar cannot slip over its head. A startled dog can frantically back out of its collar unless it is snug. If you use a retractable leash, never allow so much loose lead that your dog could suddenly jump in the path of a passing vehicle. Be prepared for the typical Min Pin rocket starts and U-turns.

If you pick a regular time of day for your walk, you will have your own personal fitness coach goading you off the couch like clockwork. Check your dog's footpads regularly for signs of abrasion, foreign bodies, tears, or blistering from hot pavement. Be considerate of those little Min Pin legs going as fast as they can go, and leave your dog at home in hot weather. Dogs are unable to cool themselves through

The lithe beauty of the miniature pinscher can best be appreciated in nature.

sweating, and heatstroke in jogging dogs is a common emergency seen by veterinarians in the summer.

The Min Pin Abroad

If your traveling takes you on the road, it may be practical to take your four-legged partner in adventure along. But there are impracticalities involved as well. Many motels do not accept pets, and many attractions have no facilities for temporary pet boarding. Most beaches, and many state parks, do not allow dogs. Dogs cannot travel on trains. There are several publications listing motels that do accept dogs (e.g., *Touring with Towser*), and many major attractions have dog boarding facilities on their grounds. Be sure to call ahead and quiz them about their safety precautions. A chain next to the highway, for example, simply will not do.

The number of establishments that accept pets decreases yearly. You can thank dog owners who seem to think their little "Poopsie" is above the law—owners who let Poopsie poop on sidewalks, beaches, and playgrounds, bark itself hoarse in the motel room, and leave behind wet spots on the carpet and chew marks on the chairs.

Luckily there still remain some places where pets are welcome. Schedule several stops in places your Min Pin can enjoy. If you are driving, bring a long retractable lead so your dog can stretch its legs safely every few hours along the way. Keep an eye out for little nature excursions, which are wonderful for refreshing both dog and owner. But always do so with a cautious eye; never risk your or your dog's safety by stopping in totally desolate locales, no matter how breathtaking the view.

Ideally your Min Pin should always ride with the equivalent of a doggy seat belt: the cage. Not only can a cage help to prevent accidents by keeping your Min Pin from using your lap as a trampoline, but if an accident does happen, the cage can save your pet's life. A cage with a padlocked door can also be useful when you need to leave the dog in the car with the windows down.

Small dogs have the advantage over large dogs that they are often able to ride in the passenger cabin of an airplane. They still must ride in a cage, and that cage must fit under the seat, but the situation is more pleasant and safer for your dog than riding in the baggage compartment. Always opt for this choice if available. Ask when making reservations what type of cage you must have. If you must ship a dog by itself, it is better to ship "counter-to-counter" than as regular air cargo. Make sure the cage is secure, and for good measure put an elastic "bungy" band around the cage door. Don't feed your dog before traveling. The cage should have a small dish that can be

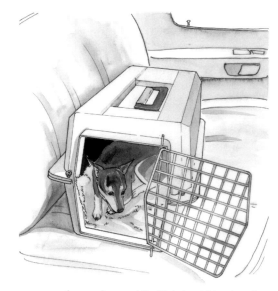

A cage is your Min Pin's best friend on the road.

attached to the door. The night before the trip, fill it with water and freeze it; as it melts during the flight, the dog will have water that otherwise would have spilled out during the loading process. Also include a large chew bone to occupy your jet-setter. Be sure to line the cage with soft, absorbent material, preferably something that can be thrown away if soiled.

Whether you will be spending your nights at a motel, campground, or even a friend's home, always have your dog on its very best behavior. Ask beforehand if it will be OK for you to bring your Min Pin. Have your dog clean and parasite-free. Do not allow your dog to run helter-skelter through the homes of friends. Bring your dog's own clean blanket or bed, or, better yet, its cage. Your Min Pin will appreciate the familiar place to sleep. Even though your dog may be used to sleeping on furniture at home, a proper guest stays on the floor when visiting. Walk and walk your dog (and clean up after it) to make sure no accidents occur inside. If they do, clean them immediately. Don't leave any surprises for your hosts! Never, never leave your dog unattended in a strange place. The dog's perception is that you have left and forgotten it; it either barks or tries to dig its way out through the doors and windows in an effort to find you, or becomes upset and relieves itself on the carpet. Always remember that anyone who allows your dog to spend the night is doing so with a certain amount of trepidation; make sure your Min Pin is so well behaved that your friends invite both of you back.

Your Min Pin should have its own travel case that should include your first aid kit, heartworm preventive and any other medications, food and water bowls, some dog biscuits and chewies, flea spray, a flea comb, a brush, a change of bedding, short and long leashes, a sweater, a flashlight, plastic baggies or other poop disposal means, moist towelettes, paper towels, and food. Besides the regular tags, your dog should wear identification indicating where you could be reached while on your trip, or including the address of someone you know will be at home. Bring a recent color photo in case your Min Pin somehow gets lost. Also bring health and rabies certificates. A jug of water from home can be a big help, as many dogs are very sensitive to changes in water and can develop diarrhea.

With a little foresight, you may find your Min Pin to be the most entertaining and enjoyable travel companion you could invite along. And don't be surprised if you find your Min Pin nestled in your suitcase as soon as you start packing!

Even if the only trip you take with your Min Pin is around the block, for the sake of dog ownership in the

Nobody likes to step in dog poop! Don't take your dog in public if you can't take responsibility for its droppings.

A leash is your Min Pin's safety line outdoors.

This chocolate has her own ideas about travel, and loves the biker life.

future, maintain the same high standards that you would if traveling.

• Always clean up after your dog. Carry a little plastic bag for disposal later.

• Don't let your dog run loose where it could bother picnickers, bicyclists, joggers, or children.

• Never let your dog bark unchecked.

• Never let your dog jump up on people.

• Never take a chance of your dog biting anybody.

• Don't allow your Min Pin to lunge at other dogs.

The Mannered Min Pin

The Min Pin Good Citizen

In recent years, there have been an increasing number of laws passed in reaction to the increasing public perception of dogs as ill-mannered, destructive, and dangerous. In an effort to encourage well-mannered, trustworthy dogs, the AKC developed the Canine Good Citizen program, in which such dogs are formally recognized with the Canine Good Citizen (CGC) designation. To pass the CGC test, all your Min Pin must demonstrate is that it will walk quietly with you around other dogs and people; sit for examination; not jump up on, act aggressively toward, or shy from someone who greets you; and stay in place without barking. The CGC is perhaps the most important title that your Min Pin can earn. The most magnificent champion in the show ring is no credit to its breed if it is not a good public citizen in the real world. Every CGC dog promotes goodwill toward dogs when it appears in public. But even if you have no desire to earn a title for your dog, you owe it to yourself, your dog, and your friends to teach your Min Pin these same essential good manners. But before you can teach your Min Pin these essentials, you must teach yourself the essentials of good training techniques.

Miniature Maneuvering

A big problem when training a little dog is how to guide and correct it. If you bend down to position your Min Pin every time you want it to sit, you will probably have a bad back before you have a sitting dog. Try some of these small dog solutions:

• Teach stationary exercises on a tabletop or other raised surface. This allows you to have eye contact with your dog and gives you a better vantage from which to help your dog learn.
• To train your dog at your feet, extend your arm length with a back scratcher, with which to guide and even pet your dog without having to bend over.
• A leash that comes from several feet overhead has virtually no guiding ability whatsoever. You need a lower pivot point for the leash in relation to the dog, and you can achieve this by what is called a "solid leash." This is simply a hollow, light tube, such as PVC pipe, about 3 feet (0.9m) long, through which you string your leash.

Every good Min Pin should know how to sit on command.

HOW-TO:
Training Like an Expert

There are certain rules that every good trainer should know:

Dog owners are not dog experts: Ignore your well-meaning friends' and neighbors' advice on how to train dogs! Everybody claims to be an authority, but very few people have a clue about the right way to train a dog, yet alone a Min Pin.

Your Min Pin hasn't read the book: Don't be discouraged when things don't go as smoothly as outlined in a book or in a class. They seldom do. Just remember: Be consistent, firm, gentle, realistic, and, most of all, patient.

Be consistent: Sometimes the puppy can be awfully cute when it misbehaves, or sometimes your hands are full, and sometimes you just aren't sure what you want from your Min Pin. But lapses in consistency are ultimately unfair to the dog. If you let the pup out of its crate because it whines "just this one time," you have taught the pup that although whining may not always result in freedom, you never know, it just might pay off tonight. In other words, *you* have taught the pup to whine.

Say what you mean and mean what you say: Your dog takes its commands literally. If you have taught that "Down" means to lie down, then what must the dog think when you yell "Down" to make it stop jumping up on you when you return home? If "Stay" means not to move until given a release word, and you say "Stay here" as you leave the house for work, do you really want your dog to sit by the door all day until you get home?

Think like a dog: In many ways, dogs are like young children; they act to gratify themselves, and they often do so without thinking ahead to consequences. But unlike young children, dogs cannot understand human language (except for those words you teach them), so you cannot explain to them that their actions of five minutes earlier were bad. Dogs live in the present; if you punish them, they can only assume it is for their behavior at the time of punishment. So if you discover a mess, then drag your dog to it from its nap in the other room, and then scold, the impression to the dog will be that either it is being scolded for napping or that its owner is mentally unstable. Remember, timing is everything in a correction. If you discover your dog in the process of having an "accident," and snatch the dog up and deposit it outside, and then yell "No," your dog can only conclude that you have yelled "No" to it for eliminating outside. Correct timing would be "No," quickly take the dog outside, and then praise it once it eliminates outside. In this way you have corrected the dog's undesired behavior and helped the dog understand desired behavior.

Correct and be done with it: Owners sometimes try to make this "a correction the dog will remember" by ignoring the dog for the rest of the day. The dog may indeed remember that its owner ignored it, but it will not remember why. Again, the dog can only relate its present behavior to your actions.

Never rough: Such methods as striking, shaking, choking, and hanging have been touted by some (stupid) trainers: Do not try them! They are extremely dangerous, counterproductive, and cruel; they have no place in the training of a beloved family member. Min Pins are a sensitive breed, both mentally and physically, and seldom require anything but the mildest of corrections. A direct stare with a harsh "No!" should be all that is required in most cases.

Name, command, action! The first ingredient in any command is your dog's name. You probably spend a good deal of your day talking, with very few words intended as commands for your dog. So, warn your dog that this talk is directed toward it. Many trainers make the mistake of simultaneously saying the command word *at the same time* that they are placing the dog into position. *This is incorrect.* The command comes immediately *before* the desired action or position. The crux of training is anticipation: The dog comes to anticipate that after hearing a command, it will be induced to perform some action, and it will eventually perform this action without further assistance from you. On the other hand, when the command and action come at the same time, not only does the dog tend to pay more attention to your action of placing it in position, and less attention to the command word, but the command word loses its predictive value for the dog.

Once is enough: Repeating a word over and over, or shouting it louder and louder, never helped anyone, dog or human, understand what is expected of the individual. Your Min Pin is not hard of hearing.

Train before meals: Your puppy will work better if its stomach is not full, and will be more responsive to treats if you use them as rewards. Never try to train a sleepy, tired, or hot Min Pin.

Happy endings: Begin and end each training session with something the dog can do well. And keep sessions short and fun—no longer than 10 to 15 minutes. Dogs have short attention spans and you will notice that after about 15 minutes, their performance will begin to suffer unless a lot of play is involved. To continue to train a tired or bored dog will result in the training of bad habits, resentment in the dog, and frustration for the trainer. Especially when training a young puppy, or when you only have one or two different exercises to practice, quit while you are ahead! Keep your Min Pin wanting more, and you will have a happy, willing, obedience partner.

Food is forever: There is nothing wrong with using food as a reward *as long as you intend to continue using it*

The most effective corrections are stern and consistent, but never rough.

throughout the dog's life. If you train a dog using food to tell it that it has done well, and then quit rewarding it with food, the impression to the dog is that it has no longer done well. It may eventually quit performing altogether under these circumstances. If you do use food, precede it with praise; that is, praise, then give a tidbit. Also, don't reward with food every time; keep the dog wondering if this will be the time with the tidbit payoff (the slot machine philosophy of dog training). That way, when you can't reward with a tidbit, your Min Pin will not be surprised and will continue to perform in the absence

of food for comparatively long periods. Of course, the advantage of using praise rather than food is that you never can be caught without praise available.

Too much of a good thing: There is such a thing as overpraising a dog throughout the day. Think of it this way: if you spend the day praising and petting your Min Pin just for breathing, why should it work for your praise later when it can get it for free? Certainly you should praise, pet, and love your Min Pin, but in some cases of disobedience such "handouts" must be curtailed. Such overindulged Min Pins must learn the value of praise by earning it.

To teach your dog to catch, toss a tidbit in an arc toward its muzzle; when it doesn't catch it, grab the tidbit before your Min Pin can snatch it. Eventually it will realize that it must catch the treat in midair to beat you to it.

A backscratcher and a solid leash guide made from a hollow tube will both help when training your small dog at floor level.

• Never grab at a Min Pin; let it approach you.
• Never reach to take a Min Pin out of somebody else's arms.
• When handing a Min Pin to someone, hand it to them backwards, so it is facing away from them.
• Unlike in humans, where direct eye contact is seen as a sign of sincerity, staring a dog directly in the eye is interpreted by the dog as a threat. It can cause a fearful dog to bite out of what it perceives as self-defense, and is responsible for many dog bites.

Cocky Min Pins are sometimes known to challenge strange dogs when good sense should tell them they are overmatched. Keeping your Min Pin on-lead and out of reach of other dogs is the best prevention. More problematic is the case where two dogs that live together do not get along. Dogs may be vying for dominance, and fights will occur until one dog emerges as the clear victor. But even in cases where one dog is dominant, fights may erupt when both are competing for the owner's attention. The dominant dog expects to get that attention before the subordinate, but being a fair-minded owner, one tends to give attention equally, or to even favor the "underdog." This can be interpreted by the dominant dog as an uprising by the subordinate dog, who is then attacked. This is one case where playing favorites (to the dominant dog) will actually be a favor to the subordinate dog in the long run!

• To prevent a small dog from sitting or lying down, loop part of your regular leash around its belly and hold onto that part, so you have a convenient "handle."

Besides the back scratcher and solid leash, equipment for training should include a 6-foot (1.8m) and a 15-foot (4.6m) light-weight lead. For puppies (as well as shy or easily trained dogs), it is convenient to use one of the lightweight adjustable size show leads. A tough adult can be outfitted with a small link chain choke collar. The latter has a truly unfortunate name, as it should never be used to choke your miniature pinscher. The proper way to administer a correction with a choke collar is with a gentle snap, then immediate release. If you think of the point of the correction as being to startle (rather than to choke) the dog by the sound of the chain links moving, you will be correcting with the right level of force, and won't risk jerking your Min Pin off its feet. The choke collar is placed on the dog so that the ring with the lead attached comes up around the left side of the dog's neck, and through the other ring. If put on backward, it will not release itself after being tightened (because you will be on the right side of your dog for most training). The choke collar should *never* be left on your Min Pin after a training session; there are too many tragic cases where a choke collar really did earn its name after being snagged on a fence, bush, or even a playmate's tooth.

What Every Good Min Pin Should Know:

Sit: Because Min Pins spend so much of their lives looking up, some of them virtually teach themselves to sit as a means of being more comfortable. But you can hasten the process by holding a tidbit above your puppy's eye level, commanding it to "Sit," and then moving the tidbit toward your pup until it is slightly behind and above its eyes. When the puppy begins to look up and bend its hind legs, praise your pet, then offer the tidbit. Repeat this, requiring the dog to bend its legs more and more until it must be sitting before receiving praise. This is a much more pleasant way for your puppy to learn its first lesson than the traditional push-pull method of teaching.

For those Min Pins that are not natural sitters, or if you do not wish to use a food reward, you will have to help the dog sit. It's easiest if you place your puppy on a table where you can easily reach it (but take care that it cannot jump off and hurt itself). After commanding "Jeepers, Sit!", push the dog backward slightly with your right hand under its chin, and simultaneously push forward, gently, behind its "knees," causing them to buckle and the dog to sit. You are, in essence, folding your Min Pin into a sit.

Stay: Next comes the "stay" command. Tell your puppy to "Sit," praise it, then say "Stay" in a soothing voice (you do not have to precede the "stay" command with the dog's name,

If you first teach your Min Pin to stay on a table top when placed there, subsequent lessons can be taught without constantly bending down to Min Pin level.

because you should already have the dog's attention on you). You should be in the same position that you always have been when teaching the "sit," either beside or directly in front of the dog, or with the dog on the table. If your Min Pin attempts to get up or lie down, gently place it back into position. After only a few seconds, give a release word ("OK!") and praise lavishly. After the dog is staying reliably, change your position relative to it.

Be careful not to smash your little dog into place when teaching the sit.

HOW-TO:
Dealing with the Misbehaving Min Pin

Min Pins are known mischief makers, and indeed, this is one of the endearing traits of the breed. But often Min Pin misbehavior causes problems for the dog's family or itself, sometimes creating an intolerable situation. Yet many of these problems can be avoided or cured. But if a problem does arise that you are unable to solve, consult your veterinarian. Some problems have physiological bases that can be treated. Also, your veterinarian may refer you to a specialist in canine behavior problems.

Hyperactivity: Well, what did you expect? Try to channel your dog's energy with set times for walks, games, and obedience. In severe cases, you may wish to consult with your dog's breeder, other Min Pin owners, or your veterinarian. If they agree your dog is simply a normal Min Pin, you can either wait for age to slow it down, or find it a home with

Barking is a handy trait—up to a point.

somebody already familiar and happy with Min Pin mania.

Barking: Having a Min Pin doorbell is rather handy, but there is a difference between a dog that will warn you of a suspicious stranger and one that will warn you of a falling leaf. Allow your Min Pin to bark momentarily at strangers, and then call it to you and praise it for quiet behavior, distracting it with an obedience exercise if need be.

Isolated dogs will often bark as a means of getting attention and alleviating loneliness. Even if the attention gained includes punishment, the dog will continue to bark in order to obtain the temporary presence of the owner. The simplest solution is to move the dog's domain to a less isolated location. If this is not possible, the pup's quiet behavior must be rewarded by the owner's presence, working up to gradually longer and longer periods. The distraction of a special chew toy, given only at bedtime, may help alleviate barking. The pup that must spend the day home alone is a greater challenge. Again, the simplest solution is to change the situation, perhaps by adding another animal—a good excuse to get two Min Pins! But warning: Min Pins also like to bark when playing!

If all else fails, and your Min Pin's barking is creating a serious problem, surgical debarking may be a kinder solution than constant reprimands or perhaps even having to find a new home.

Digging and chewing: Many a Min Pin owner has returned home to a scene of carnage, and suspected that some mad dog must have broken into the house

When left alone, even a Min Pin can wreak havoc on a home.

and gone berserk; after all, those little Min Pin teeth and paws could never wreak such havoc! Min Pins may be small, but they're quick, and a determined Min Pin can do its share of home destruction when left alone.

The best way to deal with these dogs is to provide both physical interaction (such as chasing a ball) and mental interaction (such as practicing a few simple obedience commands) on a daily basis.

More commonly, destructive behavior in an adult dog is due to separation anxiety. Most owners, upon returning home to such ruination, believe the dog is "spiting" them for leaving it, and punish the dog. Unfortunately, punishment is ineffective because it actually increases the anxiety level of the dog, as it comes to both look forward to and dread its owner's return.

The proper therapy is treatment of the dog's fear of being left alone. This is done by separating the dog for very short periods of time and gradually working to longer periods, taking care to never allow the dog to become anxious during any session. This is complicated when you *must* leave the dog for long periods during the conditioning program. In these cases, the part of the house in which the dog is left for long periods should be different from the part in which the conditioning sessions take place; the latter location should be the location where you wish to leave the dog after conditioning is completed.

In either case, when you return home, no matter what the condition of the house, greet the dog calmly or even ignore it for a few minutes, to emphasize the point that being left was really no big deal. Then have the dog perform a simple trick or obedience exercise so that you have an excuse to praise it. It takes a lot of patience, and often a whole lot of self-control, but it's not fair to you or your dog to let this situation continue.

House soiling: There are many reasons why a dog might soil the house. Commonly, the dog was never completely housebroken to start with, and so you must begin housebreaking anew. Sometimes a housebroken dog will be forced to soil the house because of a bout of diarrhea, and afterward will con-

Regular play sessions can help alleviate destruction due to boredom, but allow the dog time to calm down before leaving. Never get a dog excited and then leave it with only your furniture to play with.

Sometimes it's better to ignore the dog than to either greet it like a long lost friend or punish it.

tinue to soil in the same area. If this happens, restrict that area from the dog, and revert to basic housebreaking lessons once again. Submissive dogs may urinate upon greeting you; punishment only makes this "submissive urination" worse. For these dogs, keep greetings calm, don't bend over or otherwise dominate the dog, and usually this can be outgrown. Some dogs defecate or urinate due to the stress of separation anxiety; you must treat the anxiety to cure the symptom. Older dogs may simply not have the bladder control that they had as youngsters; paper training or a doggy door is the best solution for them. Older spayed females may "dribble"; ask your veterinarian about estrogen supplementation, which may help. And even younger dogs may have lost control due to an infection. Male dogs may "lift their leg" inside of the house as a means of marking it as theirs. Castration will usually solve this problem; otherwise diligent deodorizing and the use of some dog-deterring odorants (available at pet stores) may help.

Fearfulness: Despite their generally fearless attitude, Min

Pins can develop phobias and other fears. Never push your Min Pin into situations that might overwhelm it. A program of gradual desensitization, with the dog exposed to the frightening person or thing and then rewarded for calm behavior, is time consuming but the best way to alleviate any fear.

Never coddle your dog when it acts afraid, because it reinforces the behavior. It is always useful if your Min Pin knows a few simple commands; performing these exercises correctly gives you a reason to praise the dog and also increases the dog's sense of security because it knows what is expected of it.

Aggression: Min Pin teeth are not all that miniature, and can wreak considerable damage on human skin. The best cure for aggression is prevention, and the best prevention is to raise your Min Pin with kindness, gentleness, and firmness, not encouraging biting or displays of dominance. Expose the pup to kind strangers from a young age, and make these interactions pleasurable. Teach your Min Pin to look forward to guests and children by rewarding proper behavior, such as sitting and staying, in their presence, and by having them offer the dog a treat. A drastic measure is to withhold attention from the dog except in the presence of guests or the baby, so that the dog associates being with them as something that brings itself attention and rewards. Of course, it should hardly be mentioned that no baby or child should be allowed to play roughly with or tease your Min Pin.

If you have been beside your dog, step out (starting with your right foot) and turn to stand directly in front of it. Again tell the dog to stay, and gently prevent it from moving. Work up to longer times, and then back away and repeat the process. If you have been training on a table, you need to make the transition to the floor before backing away from the dog. Eventually you should be able to walk confidently away to longer and longer distances, and for longer and longer times. The point is not to push your dog to the limit, but to let it succeed. To do this you must be very patient, and you must increase your times and distances in very small increments. Keep in mind that young puppies cannot be expected to sit for more than 30 seconds at most. When the dog does move out of position, return and calmly place it back, repeating "Stay"; then return to your position, then return to the dog while it is still staying so that you can praise. Many trainers make the mistake of staring intently at their dog during the "stay," but this is perceived by the dog as a threat and often intimidates it so that it squirms out of position.

Calling your puppy with exuberance will help it to learn to come quickly and eagerly.

Come: When both "Sit" and "Stay" are mastered, you are ready to introduce "Come." Your puppy probably already knows how to come; after all, it comes when it sees you with the food bowl, or perhaps with the leash or ball. You may have even used the word "Come" to get its attention then; if so, you have a head start. You want your puppy to respond to "Jeepers, Come" with the same enthusiasm as though you were setting down its supper; in other words, "Come" should always be associated with good things.

Never have your dog come to you and then scold it for something it has done. In the dog's mind it is being scolded for coming, not for any earlier misdeed.

To teach the command "Come," have your Min Pin sit, and with leash attached, command "Stay" and step out to the end of the leash and face your dog. This stay will be a little different for your puppy, as you will drop to your knees, open your arms, and invite it with an enthusiastic "Jeepers, Come!" This is obviously not an exercise for tabletop training. An unsure pup can be coaxed with a tug on the lead or the sight of a tidbit. Remember to really praise; after all, you have enticed your pet to break the "stay" command, and your pup may be uneasy about that. During the training for "Come," it is not unusual for there to be some regression in the performance of "Stay" due to confusion; just be gentle, patient, and consistent and this will sort itself out.

The next step is to again place the pup in the "sit/stay," walk to the end of the lead, call "Jeepers, Come," and quickly back away several steps, coaxing the dog to you. Eventually you can go to a longer line, and walk quickly backward as far as your equilibrium will allow. This encourages the pup to come at a brisk pace; in fact, most dogs will regard this as an especially fun game! Of course, in real life the dog is seldom sitting when you want it to come, so once it understands what you mean by come, allow the pup to walk on-lead, and at irregular intervals call "Jeepers, Come," run backward, and when your pet reaches you, be sure to praise. Finally, attach a longer line to the pup, allow it to meander about, and in the midst of its investigations, call, walk backward, and praise.

"Come" is the most important command your dog will ever learn. As your dog gets older you will want to practice the command in the presence of distractions, such as other leashed dogs, unfamiliar people, cats, and cars. Always practice on-lead. If it takes a tidbit as a reward to get your Min Pin motivated, then this is an instance where you should use an occasional food reward. Coming on command is more than a cute trick; it could save your Min Pin's life.

Down: When you need your Min Pin to stay in one place for any long periods of time, it is best for it to be left in a "down/stay." Begin teaching the "down" command with the dog in the sitting position. If you are using food rewards, command "Jeepers, Down," then show your pet a tidbit and move the treat below its nose toward the ground. If it reaches down to get the treat, give the tidbit to the dog. Repeat, requiring your pet to reach farther down (without lifting its rear from the ground) until it has to lower its elbows to the ground. You can help it out here by reaching over it and easing its front legs out in front of it.

If you do not wish to use food rewards, again start with the dog sitting, command "Jeepers, Down," then place your left hand over its shoulders and with your right hand gently grasp both front legs and ease it to the ground. Never try to cram your dog into the "down" position, which could

Down must be taught gently or you risk frightening the dog.

not only cause injuries, but could scare a submissive dog and cause a dominant dog to resist.

Practice the "down/stay" just as you did the "sit/stay." In fact, your dog now has quite a repertoire of behaviors that you can combine in different ways to combat boredom. The only thing left for any well-behaved Min Pin is the ability to walk politely on-lead.

Heel: Although in many public situations it is safer to carry your Min Pin, your dog should still know how to walk nicely on a leash. An untrained Min Pin on a leash can actually be more dangerous to its owner than are many large dogs, because a Min Pin can

Proper heel position keeps the dog out of harm's way as you go about your business.

45

dart underfoot and cause its owner to trip. It is also a danger to itself, because it can be stepped on if it gets out of position. So more than most breeds, it is essential that a miniature pinscher be trained to "heel" position.

The first step is to introduce your puppy to the leash, using the lightweight show-type lead. If you have followed this training sequence, your pup should already be acquainted with the leash at least by the time it has learned "Come." Still, walking alongside of you on-lead is a new experience for a young puppy, and many will freeze in their tracks once they discover their freedom is being violated. In this case, do not simply drag the pup along, but coax it with praise, and if need be, food, until it's walking somewhere, anywhere. When the puppy follows you, praise and reward. In this way, the pup comes to realize that following you while walking on-lead pays off.

Once your Min Pin walks confidently on-lead, it is time to ask for more. Using the solid leash, have your dog sit in "heel" position; that is, on your left side with its neck next to and parallel with your leg. Say "Jeepers, Heel" and step off with your left foot first (remember that you stepped off on your right foot when you left your dog on a "stay"; if you are consistent, the foot that moves first will provide an eye-level cue for your little dog). During your first few practice sessions you will keep your pet on a short lead, holding it in "heel" position, and of course praising it. When you stop, have your pet sit. Although some trainers advocate letting the dog lunge to the end of the lead and then snapping it back, such an approach is unfair if you haven't shown the dog what is expected of it at first, and such methods are not appropriate for a miniature pinscher. Nor is the suggestion of allowing the dog to get in front

of you and then stepping on the lead. That's not safe for either of you! Instead, after a few sessions of showing the dog "heel" position, give it a little more loose lead; if it stays in "heel" position, praise; more likely it will not, in which case pull it back to position with a quick gentle snap of the lead, then release. If, after a few days of practice, your dog still seems oblivious to your efforts, turn unexpectedly several times; teach your dog that it is its responsibility to keep an eye on you.

Keep up a good pace; too slow a pace gives dogs time to sniff, to look all around and in general become distracted; a brisk pace will focus the dog's attention upon you and generally aid training. As you progress, you will want to add some right, left, and about-turns, and walk at all different speeds. Then practice in different areas (still always on-lead) and around different distractions. Vary your routine to combat boredom, and keep training sessions short. Adult dogs should be taught that heeling is not the time to relieve themselves.

Trick and Treat

The only drawback to teaching basic good manners is that such feats as sitting and staying are not likely to amaze your friends. If you would like to show off your little genius to the neighbors, you'll need a good old-fashioned dog trick. Tricks such as rolling over, playing dead, catching, sitting up, jumping the stick, and speaking are easy to teach using the same training methods as you used for basic obedience. In fact, tricks can be easier to teach, because they are almost always taught with the aid of a treat. You will find that your particular dog is more apt to perform in ways that make some tricks easier than others to teach. Most miniature pinschers are easy to teach to "speak"; wait until it appears your dog will bark, say "speak," and then reward with a treat after the bark. A dog that likes to lie on its back is a natural for "roll over"; give the command when the dog is already on its back, then guide the dog the rest of the way over with a treat. Next start with the dog on its side, then when it is lying on its belly, and finally from a stand. Work gradually to shape the desired final behavior. If your dog can physically do it, you can teach it when to do it.

Min Pin Mental Giants

Is your Min Pin "gifted?" Perhaps you and your dog have enjoyed your training sessions and would like to pursue higher education, as well as practice around distractions and discuss problems with people who have similar interests. Most cities have dog clubs or individuals that conduct obedience classes. The AKC or your local Humane Society can direct you to them. You might also contact one of the miniature pinscher breed clubs and ask for names of Min Pin obedience enthusiasts in your area. Attend a local obedience trial (contact the AKC for date and location) and ask local owners of happy working dogs (especially Min Pins!) where they train. Be aware that not all trainers may understand the Min Pin psyche, and not all classes may be right for you and your Min Pin. You may wish to visit a class first without your dog in order to evaluate whether you would be comfortable with their techniques.

The Mightiest Min Pins

If your Min Pin is well behaved and enjoys showing off or meeting new people, you and your dog have a wonderful opportunity to bring joy to others. Studies have shown that pet ownership increases life expectancy and even the simple act of petting animals can lower blood pressure. Yet many of the people who could most benefit from such interaction have no access to pets, either because they can no longer care for a pet or because they are hospitalized. The result is particularly sad for lonely elderly people who may have relied upon the companionship of a pet throughout most of their independent years. Now nursing home residents and hospitalized children have come to look forward to visits by dogs and other pets. These dogs must be meticulously well mannered and well groomed; to be registered as a Certified Therapy Dog, a dog must demonstrate that it is obedient and responds to strangers in an outgoing, yet gentle, manner. With its natural spark and joie de vivre, the miniature pinscher is bound to liven up any room. Such a little Min Pin would indeed be a giant among dogs.

Miniature Pinscher Nutrition

A Weighty Subject

A recent survey of Min Pin breeders listed obesity as a major problem in the breed. It's difficult to believe that these lithe balls of fire couldn't burn off every calorie they ingest, but apparently many Min Pins go about the practice of eating with the same gusto as they attack every other daily adventure. However, as Min Pins grow older, they do slow down and if their owners continue to feed them the same amounts as they did when younger, then obesity can result. The Min Pin can be demanding, and soft-hearted owners have difficulty not handing over tasty morsels. But there's also a problem involved when feeding a small dog: little dogs need only a little food, and when little dogs

Your adult Min Pin will be the product of what you feed it as a youngster.

are given a lot of food they cannot remain little! Because only a little food can be given, whenever table scraps or non-doggy treats are offered, these tidbits leave little room for the balanced diet the dog needs.

Your very young puppy should be fed three or four times a day, on a regular schedule. Feed it as much as it cares to eat in about 15 minutes. From the age of three to six months, your pup should be fed three times daily, and after that, twice daily. Your adult can be fed once a day, but it is actually preferable to feed smaller meals twice a day. You can let your dog decide when to eat by leaving dry food available at all times. If you choose to let your dog "self-feed," monitor its weight to be sure it is not overindulging.

You should be able to just feel the ribs slightly when you run your hands along the rib cage, and there should be a good indication of a waistline, both when viewed from above and from the side. A dog with its back-bones or hipbones clearly visible is underweight; one with a dimple at the tail base or a roll of fat over the withers is overweight; one with a shape like a football is obese.

If your Min Pin is overweight, feed one of the many low calorie foods on the market rather than simply feeding less of a high calorie food. These foods supply about 15 percent fewer calories per pound. Special care must be taken when putting a small dog on a diet, because it has a high metabolic rate and dissipates heat easily. The miniature pinscher cannot store sufficient body fat to endure long periods of food restriction, especially in cold weather. Don't try for overnight results. If your Min Pin remains overweight, make sure family members aren't sneaking it Min Pin munchies! Finally, seek your veterinarian's opinion. Some endocrine disorders, such as hypothyroidism or Cushing's disease can cause the appearance of obesity and should be ruled out or treated. Even heart disease can lead to the false impression of being overweight.

If your Min Pin is underweight, first consult your veterinarian to make sure there isn't a problem. Then try a premium-quality high calorie dog food available from most major pet food stores. You can also try feeding puppy food; add water, milk, or canned food and heat slightly to increase aroma and palatability. Take care not to reinforce picky eating habits. Some choosy canines are created when their owners begin to spice up their food with especially tasty treats. The dog then refuses to eat unless the preferred treat is offered, and finally learns that if it refuses even that proffered treat, another even tastier enticement will be offered. Give your Min Pin a good, tasty meal, but don't succumb to Min Pin blackmail or you may be a slave to your dog's gastronomical whims for years to come. Again, some cases of poor weight are due to problems that your veterinarian must diagnose, for example, internal parasites or kidney disease.

Min Pin Din-Din

There are a number of high-quality palatable foods on the market from which to choose, but one of your first choices will be which form of food to feed: dry, moist, or canned. Dry food is the most popular, economical, and healthiest, but least palatable. The

Smarter than the average dog, Min Pins have a way of ferreting food out of any situation—even if it means stowing away in a picnic basket.

high moisture content of canned foods helps to make them tasty, but it also makes them comparatively expensive, because you are in essence buying water. A steady diet of canned food would not provide the chewing necessary to maintain dental health. In addition, a high meat content, such as often found in canned foods, tends to increase levels of dental plaque. Moist foods are popular with some dog owners, but these too cannot provide proper chewing and also have the disadvantage of being fairly expensive and loaded with sugar-based preservatives. But many dogs enjoy them so they can be a reasonable choice for use in conjunction with a high-quality dry food. They are also very convenient when traveling. Dog biscuits provide excellent chewing action, and some of the better varieties provide complete nutrition.

You and your Min Pin may have to do some shopping and compromising

Canned food is tasty, but can be expensive.

Dry food is most economical, but the least favorite of dogs.

before you settle on a food. Look for a food that your dog likes, one that creates a small volume of firm stools and results in good weight with a nice coat. Be aware of the signs of possible food allergies (loss of hair, scratching, inflamed ears). Rice and lamb-based foods are often good for dogs with food allergies, but are seldom necessary otherwise.

When changing foods you should do so gradually, mixing in progressively more and more of the new food each day for several days. One of the great mysteries of life is why a species, such as the dog, that is renown for its lead stomach and preference to eat out of garbage cans, can at the same time develop violently upset stomachs simply from changing from one high-quality dog food to another. But it happens.

Reading Dog Food Labels

The components that vary most from one brand of food to another are protein and fat percentages.

Protein: Many high-quality foods boast of being high in protein, and with good reason. Protein provides the necessary building blocks for growth and maintenance of bones and muscle, and in the production of infection-fighting antibodies. The best sources of protein are meat based, but soybeans are also a popular source. Puppies and adolescents need particularly high protein levels in their diets, which is one reason they are best fed a food formulated for their life stage. Older dogs, especially those with kidney problems, should be fed much lower levels of very high-quality protein.

Fat: Fat is the calorie-rich component of foods, and most dogs prefer the taste of foods with higher fat content. Fat is necessary to good health, aiding in the transport of important vitamins and providing energy. Dogs deficient in fat often have sparse, dry coats. A higher fat content is usually found in puppy foods, whereas obese dogs or dogs with heart problems would do well to be fed a lower fat food.

Choose a food that has a protein and fat content best suited for your dog's life stage, adjusting for any weight or health problems (there are a number of special diets available from your veterinarian especially designed for specific health problems). Also examine the list of ingredients: A good rule of thumb is that three or four of the first six ingredients should be animal derived. These tend to be more palatable and more highly digestible than plant-based ingredients; more highly digestible foods mean less stool volume and less gas problems.

Min Pin No-No's
• Chicken, pork, lamb, or fish bones. These can be swallowed and their sharp ends can pierce the stomach or intestinal walls.
• Any bone that could be swallowed whole or that could splinter. This could cause choking or intestinal blockage.
• Mineral supplements unless advised to do so by your veterinarian.
• Chocolate. Contains theobromine, which is poisonous to dogs.
• Alcohol. Small dogs can drink fatal amounts quickly.

Min Pin Maintenance

Coat and Skin Care

Even with its close hair, your Min Pin will need a short grooming session once or twice a week in order to keep its coat gleaming and healthy. Use a natural bristle brush to distribute the oils, a rubber bristle brush to remove dead hair, and a flea comb to remove fleas or fine debris.

Min Pins rarely need bathing (in fact, wiping them thoroughly with a damp sponge will work wonders), but when bathing is necessary, it is best accomplished in a sink with a spray attachment. Use warm water that would be comfortable for you if it were your bath. Place cotton balls in the dog's ears, and wash its entire body before starting on its head. Then rinse the head with a sponge, followed by the rest of the body with the spray.

You will get better results with a shampoo made for dogs. Dog skin has a pH of 7.5, whereas human skin has a pH of 5.5; bathing in a shampoo formulated for the pH of human skin can lead to scaling and irritation. Most shampoos will kill fleas even if not especially formulated as a flea shampoo, but none has any residual killing action on fleas. In addition, there are a variety of therapeutic shampoos for use with skin problems. Treatment includes moisturizing shampoos for dry scaly skin, antiseborrheic shampoos for excessive scale and dandruff, antimicrobials for damaged skin, and oatmeal-based antipruritics for itchy skin. Finally, no one should be without one of the shampoos that requires no water or rinsing. These are wonderful for puppies, emergencies, and bathing when time does not permit. When finished, dry the dog thoroughly and do not allow it to become chilled.

Skin and Coat Problems

Itchy skin most often results from flea infestation, sarcoptic mange, or allergies (to food, airborne particles, grass, or flea saliva). First make sure that not a single flea is on your dog. If scratching continues, you and your veterinarian will have to play detectives. Mange mites can be detected through skin scrapings; for allergies, you can try avoiding certain foods and environments. Often a lamb and rice-based food will bring relief. New carpeting or wet grass may be the culprit. Cortisone can bring some relief from the itching, but can cause damage to your Min Pin in the long run if used too frequently.

In some cases, hair is lost without the dog itching. Demodectic mange, thyroid deficiency, estrogen excess, ringworm, and seborrhea are all possibilities that your veterinarian can diagnose.

Blisters and brown crust on the stomach of your puppy indicate puppy impetigo. Clean the area twice daily with dilute hydrogen peroxide or surgical soap, and treat with a topical antibiotic.

Fleas: A few fleas on a little dog can make its life miserable; a lot of fleas can actually be debilitating. They leave behind a black pepperlike substance (actually flea feces) that turns red upon getting wet. Some Min Pins develop an allergic reaction to the saliva of the flea; one bite can cause

A flea comb has teeth so finely spaced that any fleas are trapped between them.

them to itch and chew for days. Flea allergies are typically characterized by loss of coat and little red bumps around the lower back and tail base.

Ticks: Ticks can carry Rocky Mountain spotted fever, Lyme disease, and, most commonly, "tick fever" (erlichiosis)—all potentially fatal diseases. Use a tissue or tweezers to remove ticks, because some diseases can be transmitted to humans. Grasp the tick as close to the skin as possible, and pull slowly and steadily, trying not to leave the head in the dog. Often a bump will remain after the tick is removed, even if you got the head. It will go away with time.

Mange mites: Min Pins are prone to two very different forms of mange. Sarcoptic mange is highly contagious, characterized by intense itching and often scaling of the ear tips, but is easily treated with insecticidal dips. Demodectic mange is not contagious and does not itch, but can be difficult to cure. It tends to run in families, and is characterized by a moth-eaten appearance, often on the face or feet; advanced cases lead to serious secondary infections. Some localized forms may go away on their own, but more widespread cases will need a special dip regime prescribed by your veterinarian. You must adhere to the dip schedule fanatically in order to effect a cure in these cases. Demodectic mange is more common in some breeds, including miniature pinschers, than in others.

Nail Care

When you can hear the pitter-patter of clicking nails, that means that with every step the nails are hitting the floor, and when this happens the bones of the foot are spread, causing discomfort and eventually splayed feet and lameness. If dewclaws are left untrimmed, they can get caught on things more easily or actually loop around and grow into the dog's leg. You must prevent this by trimming your dog's nails every week or two.

Begin by handling the feet and nails daily, and then "tipping" the ends of your puppy's nails every week, taking special care not to cut the "quick" (the central core of blood vessels and nerve endings). Many people find a scissors-type clipper easier to use on a toy dog than a guillotine nail clipper, but either type is acceptable. You may find it easiest to cut the nails with your Min Pin lying on its back in your lap, or you may have a helper hold your dog. If you look at the bottoms of the nails, you will see a solid core culminating in a hollowed nail. Cut the tip up to the core, but not beyond. On occasion, you will slip up and cause the nail to bleed. This is best stopped by styptic powder, but if this is not available, dip the nail in flour or hold it to a wet tea bag. Be ready for your Min Pin to demand an apology!

The "quick" of the nail consists of blood vessels surrounded by nerves. The nail becomes progressively less brittle as it gets closer to the quick, providing another cue about its location when cutting.

Ear Care

You should examine both inside and outside your Min Pin's ears during your grooming session. Fly bites can sometimes irritate the outer edges, and can be treated with a soothing cream.

The ears may have an accumulation of dirt and wax. This can be removed by soaking a cotton ball with mineral oil and swabbing the ear. Do not reach farther than you can see. Do not use alcohol, which can dry and irritate the ear. Avoid also ear powders, which can cake in the ear. Ear cleaners, available from your veterinarian, are the best solution for maintaining ear health. If the ear continues to have an excessive discharge, it may be due to a fungal or bacterial problem, which must be treated by your veterinarian. It could also be due to ear mites.

Ear mites: Tiny but irritating, ear mites are highly contagious and often found in puppies. Affected dogs will shake their head, scratch their ears, and carry their head sideways. There is a dark waxy buildup in the ear canal, usually of both ears. If you place some of this wax on a piece of dark paper, and have very good eyes, you may be able to see tiny white moving specks. These are the culprits. Although there are over-the-counter ear mite preparations, they can cause worse irritation. Therefore, ear mites should be diagnosed and treated by your veterinarian.

Dental Care

At around five to six months of age, your Min Pin puppy will begin to shed its baby teeth and show off new permanent teeth. Often baby teeth, especially the canines ("fangs"), are not shed, so that the permanent tooth grows in beside the baby tooth. If this condition persists for over a week, consult your veterinarian. Retained baby teeth can cause misalignment of adult teeth.

A healthy glow goes hand-in-hand with good health. The eyes, ears, and teeth should receive regular attention.

Check the way your puppy's teeth meet up; in a correct bite, the bottom incisors should touch the back of the top incisors when the mouth is closed. Deviations from this can cause chewing problems and discomfort. Extreme deviations may need to be examined by a veterinarian.

As your dog gets older, its teeth will tend to accumulate plaque. The plaque can be removed by brushing the dog's teeth once or twice weekly with a child's toothbrush and doggy toothpaste. You can also rub the teeth with hydrogen peroxide or a baking soda solution on a gauze pad to help remove tartar. Hard dog foods and chew bones are helpful, but cannot do the job on their own. If not removed, plaque will attract bacteria and minerals, which will harden into tartar. If you cannot brush, your

HOW-TO:
Making Fleas Flee

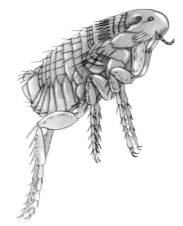

The flea can make your dog's life miserable.

Flea control can be difficult, but with a small dog there is no excuse for fleas to get the upper hand. Any flea control program must be undertaken with care, because overzealous and uninformed efforts may lead to the death of pets as well as fleas. Insecticides can be categorized as organics, natural pesticides, cholinesterase inhibitors, insect growth regulators, and systemics. Incidentally, the ultrasonic flea repelling collars have been shown to be both ineffective on fleas and irritating to dogs. Scientific studies have also shown that feeding dogs brewer's yeast, as has been advocated for years by many dog owners, is ineffective against fleas.

Organics (e.g., D-Limonene) break down the outer shell of the flea and cause death from dehydration. They are safe, but slow acting and have no residual action. Diatomaceous earth also acts on this same principle; some researchers have expressed concern that breathing its dust can be dangerous to dogs, however. This is a special concern when dealing with a dog that is as low to the ground as the Min Pin. Natural grade diatomaceous earth is probably safe; pool grade is probably not.

Natural pesticides (e.g., Pyrethrin, Permethrin, Rotenone) are relatively safe and kill fleas quickly, but have a very short residual action. They do not remain in the dog's system and so can be used frequently.

Cholinesterase inhibitors (e.g., Dursban, Diazinon, Malathion, Sevin, Carbaryl, Pro-Spot, Spotton) act on the nervous systems of fleas, dogs, and humans. They are used in yard sprays, dog sprays and dips, flea collars, and systemics. They kill effectively and have fairly good residual action. But they can poison the dog if overused, and should never be used on puppies or sick dogs. The systemics are drugs that are applied to the dog's skin for absorption into the blood, or given orally, so that the flea dies when it sucks the blood. It is extremely important that you be aware of which chemicals in your arsenal are cholinesterase inhibitors. Using a yard spray in conjunction with systemics, or some sprays and dips, or with certain worm medications that are also cholinesterase inhibitors, can be a deadly combination.

Insect growth regulators (IGRs) prevent immature fleas from maturing and have proven to be the most highly effective method for long-term flea control. Precor is the most widely used for indoor applications, but is quickly broken down by ultra-

The dog's owner must make a careful, informed choice of insecticides.

violet light. Fenoxicarb is better for outdoor use because it is resistant to ultraviolet light. IGRs are nontoxic to mammals but do tend to be expensive. A new type of IGR on the market is the nematode that eats flea larva. Studies show it to be effective and safe, but it must be reapplied regularly because the nematodes die when their food supply (the current crop of flea larva) is gone. Newest on the market is an IGR given to the dog orally once a month, available through your veterinarian.

One final warning. There is a popular product on the market that contains "deet" (diethyl-m-toluamide: the same chemical found in some human insect repellents). It has been implicated in the death of many dogs, and is not recommended for Min Pins.

The safest flea control product is the flea comb, a comb with such finely spaced teeth that it catches fleas between them. Have a cup of alcohol handy for disposing of the fleas. A cotton

Spray into corners and crevices to rid the home of fleas.

ball soaked in alcohol and applied to a flea on the dog will also result in the flea's demise.

Because only about 1 to 10 percent of your home's flea population is actually on your dog, you must concentrate on treating your home and yard. These are best treated with a combination adult flea killer and IGR. Wash all pet bedding and vacuum other surfaces regularly, and especially before applying

insecticides. Be sure that sprays reach into small crevices. Outside, cut grass short and spray in all areas except those that are never shaded (fleas do not mature in these areas).

It may not be easy, but you can win the battle. Every time you feel like giving up, consider how your Min Pin deserves to live: free of the constant itching caused by a colony of blood-sucking parasites.

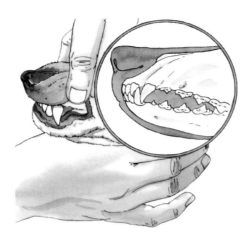

Check your Min Pin's teeth for correct scissors bite (as illustrated) and for tartar. Tooth problems can cause discomfort and serious health problems.

veterinarian can supply a cleansing solution that will help to kill plaque-forming bacteria, as well as bad breath! Neglected plaque and tartar can cause infections to form along the gum line. The infection can gradually work its way down the sides of the tooth until the entire root is undermined. The tissues and bone around the tooth erode, and the tooth finally falls out. Meanwhile, the bacteria may have been picked up by the bloodstream and carried throughout the body, causing infection in the kidneys and heart valves. Thicker tartar deposits will have to be removed with a dental scraper, possibly under anesthesia, which entails some risk in older Min Pins.

Small dogs, including Min Pins, are especially prone to tooth loss and periodontal disease. There is no such thing as doggy dentures, so help your Min Pin keep its teeth into old age by keeping its teeth sparkling throughout its life.

The Health Check

A weekly health check should be part of your grooming procedure. The health check should include examining the eyes for discharge or cloudiness; the ears for bad smell, redness, or discharge; the mouth for red swollen gums, loose teeth, or bad breath; and the skin for parasites, hair loss, or lumps. Most bumps and lumps are not cause for concern, but because there is always a possibility of cancer, they should be examined by your veterinarian. This is especially true of a sore that does not heal, or any pigmented lump that begins to grow or bleed. Observe your dog for signs of lameness or incoordination, or for behavioral change. Weigh your dog and observe whether it is putting on fat or wasting away.

In Sickness and in Health

Choosing Your Veterinarian

When choosing your veterinarian, consider availability, emergency arrangements, costs, facilities, and ability to communicate. You and your veterinarian will form a partnership that will work together to protect your Min Pin's health, so your rapport with your veterinarian is very important. Your veterinarian should listen to your observations, and should explain to you exactly what is happening with your dog. If you think your dog may have a contagious illness, inform the clinic beforehand so that you can use another entrance. Your veterinarian will be appreciative if your Min Pin is clean and under control during the examination. Warn your veterinarian if you think there is any chance that your dog may bite.

Medications

Giving medications to your Min Pin should not be difficult. For pills, open your dog's mouth and place (don't throw) the pill well to the back and in the middle of the tongue. Close the mouth and gently stroke the throat until your dog swallows. Pre-wetting capsules or covering them with cream cheese or some other food helps prevent capsules from sticking to the tongue or the roof of the mouth. For liquid medicine, tilt the head back and place the liquid in the pouch of the cheek. Then close your dog's mouth until it swallows. Always give the full course of medications prescribed by your veterinarian.

You may also need to take your dog's temperature on occasion. Use a rectal thermometer, preferably the digital type; lubricate it, and insert it about 1.5 inches (3.8cm). Do not allow your dog to sit down, or the thermometer could break. Normal temperature for a small dog is around 102°F (38.9°C). Incidentally, not only do small dogs tend to have a slightly higher body temperature than do large dogs, but they also tend to have a higher heart rate, averaging about 180 beats per minute (200 to 220 per minute for puppies).

Min Pin Preventive Medicine

The best preventive medicine is that which prevents accidents: a well-trained dog in a well-fenced yard or on a leash, and a properly Min Pin-proofed home. Other preventive steps must be taken to avoid diseases and parasites, however.

Vaccinations

Rabies, distemper, leptospirosis, canine hepatitis, parvovirus, and coronavirus are highly contagious and deadly diseases that have broken many a loving owner's heart in the past. Now that vaccinations are available for these diseases one would think they would no longer be a threat, but many dogs remain unvaccinated and continue to succumb to and spread these potentially fatal illnesses. Don't let your friend be one of them.

Puppies receive their dam's immunity through nursing in the first day of life. This is why it is important that your pup's mother be properly immunized

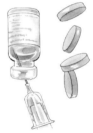

Preventive medicine will go a long way in maintaining your dog's health.

Heartworm larva are spread by mosquitoes from dog to dog. Untreated, they mature and reproduce in the infected dog's heart and can eventually cause death.

before breeding, and that your pup be able to nurse from its dam. The immunity gained from the mother will wear off after several weeks, and then the pup will be susceptible to disease unless you provide immunity through vaccinations. The problem is that there is no way to know exactly when this passive immunity will wear off, and vaccinations given before that time are ineffective. So you must re-vaccinate over a period of weeks so that your pup will not be unprotected and will receive lasting immunity. Your pup's breeder will have given the first vaccinations to your pup before it was old enough to go home with you. Bring all information about your pup's vaccination history to your veterinarian on your first visit so that the vaccination schedule can be maintained. Meanwhile, it is best not to let your pup mingle with strange dogs.

Heartworm Preventive

Wherever mosquitoes are present, dogs should be on heartworm preven-

tive. There are several types of heartworm preventive on the market; all are effective. Some are also effective in preventing many other types of worms. Ask your veterinarian when your puppy should begin taking the preventive. If you forget to give the preventive as described, and your dog is bitten by a mosquito carrying heartworm larvae, your Min Pin may get heartworms. A dog with suspected heartworms should not be given the preventive because a fatal reaction could occur. Heartworms are treatable in their early stages, but the treatment is expensive and not without risks. If untreated, heartworms can kill your dog.

Min Pin Maladies

Vomiting

Vomiting is a common occurrence that may or may not indicate a serious problem. You should consult your veterinarian immediately if your dog vomits a foul substance resembling fecal matter (indicating a blockage in the intestinal tract), blood (partially digested blood resembles coffee grounds), or if there is projectile vomiting, in which the stomach contents are forcibly ejected up to a distance of several feet. Sporadic vomiting with poor appetite and generally poor condition could indicate worms or a more serious internal disease that should also be checked by your veterinarian.

Overeating is a common cause of vomiting in puppies, especially if they follow eating with playing. Feed smaller meals more frequently if this becomes a problem. Vomiting after eating grass is common and usually of no great concern. Repeated vomiting could indicate that the dog has eaten spoiled food, undigestible objects, or may have stomach illness. Use the same home treatment as that outlined for diarrhea on the following page.

Diarrhea

Diarrhea can result from overexcitement or nervousness, a change in diet or water, sensitivity to certain foods, overeating, intestinal parasites, infectious diseases such as parvovirus or coronavirus, or ingestion of toxic substances. Bloody diarrhea, diarrhea with vomiting, fever, or other signs of toxicity, or diarrhea that lasts for more than a day should not be allowed to continue without veterinary advice.

Less severe diarrhea can be treated at home by withholding or severely restricting food and water. Ice cubes can be given to satisfy thirst. Administer a human antidiarrheal medicine in the same weight dosage as recommended for humans. A bland diet consisting of rice (flavored if need be with cooked, drained hamburger), cottage cheese, or cooked macaroni should be given for several days.

Intestinal Parasites

When you take the pup to be vaccinated, bring along a stool specimen so that your veterinarian can also check for worms. Most puppies do have worms at some point, even pups from the most fastidious breeders. This is because some types of worms become encysted in the dam's body long before she ever becomes pregnant; perhaps when she herself is a pup. Here they lie dormant and immune from worming, until hormonal changes due to her pregnancy cause them to be activated, and then they infect her babies. You may be tempted to pick up some worm medication and worm your puppy yourself. Don't. Over-the-counter wormers are largely ineffective and often more dangerous than those available through your veterinarian. Left untreated, worms can cause vomiting, diarrhea, dull coat, listlessness, anemia, and death. Some heartworm preventives also prevent most types of

intestinal worms, so that if you have a recurring problem in an older dog, they might help.

Tapeworms tend to plague some dogs throughout their lives. There is no preventive, except to diligently rid your Min Pin of fleas, because fleas can transmit tapeworms to dogs. Tapeworms look like moving flat white worms on fresh stools, or may dry up and look like rice grains around the dog's anus.

Common misconceptions about worms exist. These include:
• Misconception: A dog that is scooting its rear along the ground has worms. This is seldom the case; such a dog more likely has impacted anal sacs.
• Misconception: Feeding a dog sugar and sweets will give it worms. There are good reasons not to feed a dog

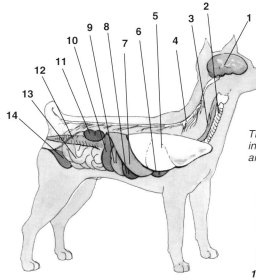

Your Min Pin's health depends upon every internal organ functioning properly, and that depends upon you recognizing the signs of dysfunction.

The major internal organs are:

1. Brain
2. Trachea
3. Esophagus
4. Spinal cord
5. Lungs
6. Heart
7. Diaphragm
8. Liver
9. Stomach
10. Spleen
11. Kidney
12. Rectum
13. Small intestine
14. Bladder

A long, active life starts with good pediatric care.

sweets, but worms have nothing to do with them.

• Misconception: Dogs should be regularly wormed every month or so. Dogs should be wormed when, and only when, they have been diagnosed with worms. No worm medication is completely without risk, and it is foolish to use it carelessly.

Impacted Anal Sacs

Dogs have two anal sacs that are normally emptied by rectal pressure during defecation. Their musky smelling contents may also be forcibly ejected when a dog is extremely frightened. Sometimes they fail to empty properly and become impacted or infected. This is more common in small dogs, obese dogs, dogs with seborrhea, and dogs that seldom have firm stools. Constant licking of the anus or scooting of the anus along the ground are characteristic signs of anal sac impaction. Not only is this an extremely uncomfortable condition for your dog, but left unattended, the impacted sacs can become infected. Your veterinarian can show you how

to empty the anal sacs yourself. Some dogs may never need to have their anal sacs expressed, but others may need regular attention.

Urinary tract diseases

If your dog drinks and urinates more than usual, it may be suffering from a kidney problem. See your veterinarian for a proper diagnosis and treatment. Although the excessive urination may cause problems in keeping your house clean or your night's sleep intact, *never* try to restrict water from a dog with kidney disease. Untreated kidney disease can lead to death. Increased thirst and urination could also be a sign of diabetes.

If your dog has difficulty or pain in urination, urinates suddenly but in small amounts, or passes cloudy or bloody urine, it may be suffering from a problem of the bladder, urethra, or prostate. Your veterinarian will need to examine your Min Pin to determine the exact nature of the problem. Bladder infections must be treated promptly to avoid the infection reaching the kidneys. A common cause of urinary incontinence in older spayed females is lack of estrogen, which can be treated. Your veterinarian should check your older male's prostate to ensure that it is not overly enlarged, which can cause problems in both urination and defecation.

Coughing

Any persistent cough should be checked by your veterinarian. Coughing irritates the throat and can lead to secondary infections if allowed to continue unchecked. There are many reasons for coughing, including allergies, but two of the most common are kennel cough and heart disease.

Kennel cough is a highly communicable airborne disease against which you can also request your dog be vaccinated. This is an especially good idea if you plan to have your dog around other dogs at training classes or while being boarded.

Heart disease can result in coughing following exercise or in the evening. Treatment with diuretics prescribed by your veterinarian can help alleviate the coughing for awhile, as can a special diet and other medications.

Eye Discharge

A watery discharge, accompanied by squinting or pawing, often indicates a foreign body in the eye. Examine under the lids and use a moist cotton swab to removed any debris. Flooding the eye with saline solution can also aid in removal. Continued tearing of the eye could be due to eyelid anomalies that irritate the cornea; if ignored, they could injure the eye to the point of causing blindness.

A thick or crusty discharge suggests conjunctivitis. Mild cases can be treated by over-the-counter preparations for humans, but if you don't see improvement within a day of treatment, your veterinarian should be consulted.

Any time your dog's pupils do not react to light or when one eye reacts differently from another, take your pet to the veterinarian immediately. It could indicate a serious ocular or neurological problem.

Limping

Puppies are especially susceptible to bone and joint injuries, and should not be encouraged to jump off of high places, walk on their hind legs, or run until exhausted. Persistent limping in puppies may result from one of several developmental bone problems, and should be checked. Both puppies and adults should be kept off of slippery floors that could cause them to lose their footing. Limping may or may not indicate a serious problem. When associated with extreme pain, fever, swelling, discoloration, deformity, or grinding or popping sounds, you

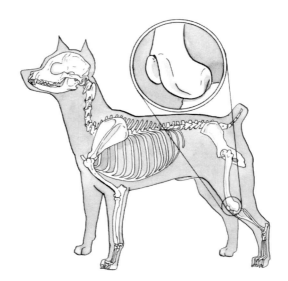

The miniature pinscher skeleton, with an enlarged view of the patella, the site of patellar luxation. Femoral head necrosis, another cause of lameness, occurs at the end of the thigh (femur) bone where it meets the pelvis.

should have your veterinarian examine your Min Pin at once. Ice packs may help minimize swelling if applied immediately after an injury. Fractures should be immobilized by splinting above and below the site of fracture (small rolled magazines work well on legs) before moving the dog. Mild lameness should be treated by complete rest; if it still persists after three days, your dog will need to be examined by its doctor. Knee injuries are common in dogs; most do not get well on their own. Avoid pain medications that might encourage the use of an injured limb. In older dogs, or dogs with a previous injury, limping is often the result of arthritis. Arthritis can be treated with aspirin, but should be done so only under veterinary supervision. Do not use ibuprofen or naproxen. Toy breeds are more prone to be affected with rheumatoid arthritis. Any time a young or middle-aged dog shows signs of

HOW-TO:
Handling Emergencies

Emergencies don't always (in fact, seldom) occur during your veterinarian's office hours. Know the phone number and location of the emergency veterinarian in your area. Make sure you always have enough fuel in your car to make it to the emergency clinic without stopping to find a gas station.

The following situations are all *life threatening emergencies*. For all cases, administer the first aid treatment outlined and seek the nearest veterinary help *immediately*. Call the clinic first so that they can prepare.

In general:
• Make sure breathing passages are open. Loosen collar and check mouth and throat.
• Be calm and reassuring. A calm dog is less likely to go into shock.
• Move the dog as little and as gently as possible.
• If the dog is in pain, it may bite. Apply a makeshift muzzle

An emergency muzzle can be fashioned by crossing a strip of cloth or your leash around the snout and tying it behind the ears.

Heat stroke is an extreme emergency.

with a bandage or tape. Do not muzzle if breathing difficulties are present.

Shock
Signs: Very pale gums, weakness, unresponsiveness, faint pulse, shivering.

Treatment: Keep the dog warm and calm; control any bleeding; check breathing, pulse, and consciousness, and treat these problems if needed.

Heat Stroke
Signs: Rapid, loud breathing; abundant thick saliva, bright red mucous membranes, high rectal temperature. Later signs: unsteadiness, diarrhea, coma.

Treatment: Immediately cover the dog with towels soaked in cold water. Place the dog in a cool room or in front of a fan. If this treatment is not possible, immerse the dog in cold water. You *must* lower your dog's body temperature quickly (but do not lower it below 100°F [37.8°C]).

Breathing Difficulties
Signs: Gasping for breath with head extended, anxiety, weakness; advances to loss of consciousness, bluish tongue

(exception: carbon monoxide poisoning causes bright red tongue).

Treatment: If not breathing, give mouth-to-nose respiration:
1. Open the dog's mouth, clear passage of secretions and foreign bodies.
2. Pull the dog's tongue forward.
3. Seal your mouth over the dog's nose and mouth, blow gently into the dog's nose for three seconds, then release.
4. Continue until the dog breathes on its own.

If due to drowning, turn the dog upside down, holding it by the hind legs, so that water can run out of its mouth. Then administer mouth-to-nose respiration, with the dog's head positioned lower than its lungs.

Hypoglycemia (Low Blood Sugar)
Signs: Appears disoriented, weak, staggering. May appear blind, and muscles may twitch. Later stages lead to convulsions, coma, and death.

Treatment: Give food, or honey or syrup mixed with warm water.

Poisoning
Signs: Varies according to poison, but commonly include vomiting, convulsions, staggering, collapse.

Treatment: Call your veterinarian and give as much information as possible. Induce vomiting (*except* in the cases outlined on the next page) by giving either hydrogen peroxide, salt water, or mustard and water. Treat for shock and get to the veterinarian at once. Be prepared for convulsions or respiratory distress.

Do *not* induce vomiting if the poison was an acid, alkali, petroleum product, solvent, cleaner, or tranquilizer, or if a sharp object was swallowed; also do *not* induce vomiting if the dog is severely depressed, convulsing, comatose, or if over two hours have passed since ingestion. If the dog is *not* convulsing or unconscious: dilute the poison by giving milk, vegetable oil, or egg whites.

Convulsions

Signs: Drooling, stiffness, muscle spasms.

Treatment: Prevent your dog from injuring itself on furniture or stairs. Remove other dogs from the area. Treat for shock.

Snakebites

Signs: Swelling, discoloration, pain, fang marks, restlessness, nausea, weakness.

Treatment: Restrain the dog and keep it quiet. Be able to describe the snake. If you can't get to the veterinarian, apply a tourniquet between the bite and the heart tight enough to prevent blood from returning to the heart. Make vertical parallel

Apply pressure to wounds. Do not remove bandages even if they became saturated; instead, add new bandages on top of them.

cuts (deep enough for blood to ooze out of) through the fang marks and suction out the blood (do not use your mouth if you have any open sores).

Open Wounds

Signs: Consider wounds to be an emergency if there is profuse bleeding, if extremely deep, if open to chest cavity, abdominal cavity, or head.

Treatment: Control massive bleeding first. Cover the wound with a clean dressing and apply pressure; apply more dressings over the others until bleeding stops. Also elevate the wound site, and apply a cold pack to the site. If an extremity, apply pressure to the closest pressure point as follows:

• For a front leg: inside of the front leg just above the elbow.
• For a rear leg: inside of the thigh where the femoral artery crosses the thighbone.
• For the tail: underside of the tail close to where it joins the body.

Use a tourniquet only in life-threatening situations and when all other attempts have failed. Check for signs of shock.

Sucking chest wounds: Place a sheet of plastic or other nonporous material over the hole and bandage it to make an airtight seal.

Abdominal wounds: Place warm, wet, sterile dressing over any protruding internal organs; cover with a bandage or towel. Do not attempt to push organs back into the dog.

Head wounds: Apply gentle pressure to control bleeding. Monitor for loss of consciousness or shock and treat accordingly.

Deep Burns

Signs: Charred or pearly white skin; deeper layers of tissue exposed.

Treatment: Cool burned area with cool packs, towels soaked in ice water, or by immersing in cold water. If over 50 percent of the dog is burned, do not immerse as this increases the likelihood of shock. Cover with a clean bandage or towel to avoid contamination. Do not apply pressure; do not apply ointments. Monitor for shock.

Electrical Shock

Signs: Collapse, burns inside mouth.

Treatment: Before touching the dog, disconnect the plug or cut power; if that cannot be done immediately, use a wooden pencil, spoon, or broom handle to knock cord away from the dog. Keep your dog warm and treat for shock. Monitor breathing and heartbeat.

Again, the procedures outlined above are first aid only. They do not take the place of the emergency veterinary clinic. Nor is the above list a complete catalog of emergency situations. Situations not described can usually be treated with the same first aid as for humans.

You should maintain a first aid/medical kit for your Min Pin, which should contain at least: a rectal thermometer, scissors, tweezers, sterile gauze dressings, a self-adhesive bandage, an instant cold compress, anti-diarrhea medication, ophthalmic ointment, soap, antiseptic skin ointment, hydrogen peroxide, first aid instructions, and veterinarian and emergency clinic numbers.

arthritis, especially in a joint that has not been previously injured, it should be examined by its veterinarian.

Some Min Pins are prone to patellar luxation (displaced kneecap), especially when they are young. In most dogs, the patella is held in its proper position by a deep groove, but if the groove is too shallow you can actually push the patella out of place to either the inside or outside of the knee. When out of place, the dog cannot straighten its leg and will tend to hold the affected leg up for a few steps at a time, or all of the time, until the patella pops back into place. While standing, it may appear either knock-kneed or bowlegged. This condition can be surgically repaired; if it is present in a puppy, such repair should be done by a few months of age, before the leg becomes permanently deformed.

The Very Mature Min Pin

With good care and good luck your Min Pin will mature and eventually, grow old. Pat yourself on the back for a job well done, but be ready to be twice as diligent in caring for your dog now. When does old age start? It varies between breeds and individuals, with the average Min Pin showing signs of aging at a much older age than do most larger breeds. You may first notice that it sleeps longer and more soundly than it did as a youngster. Upon awakening, it is slower to get going and may be stiff at first. It may be less eager to play and more content to lie in the sun (in other words, it may begin to act like a normal dog!). Some dogs become cranky and less patient, especially when dealing with puppies or boisterous children.

Older dogs may seem to ignore their owners' commands, but this may be the result of hearing loss. The slight haziness that appears in the older dog's pupils is normal and has minimal effect upon vision, but some dogs, especially those with diabetes, may develop cataracts. These can be removed by a veterinary ophthalmologist if they are severe.

Both physical activity and metabolic rates decrease in older animals, meaning that they require fewer calories to maintain the same weight. It is important to keep your older dog active. Older dogs that continue to be fed the same as when they were young risk becoming obese; such dogs have a greater risk of cardiovascular and joint problems.

Older dogs should be fed several small meals instead of one large meal, and should be fed on time. There are a variety of reduced calorie, low protein senior diets on the market. But most older dogs do not require a special diet unless they have a particular medical need for it (e.g., obesity: low calorie; kidney failure: low protein; heart failure: low sodium). Dogs with these problems may require special prescription dog foods, available from your veterinarian, that better address their needs.

Like people, dogs lose skin moisture as they age, and though dogs don't wrinkle, their skin can become dry and itchy as a result. Regular brushing can stimulate oil production. Older dogs tend to have a stronger body odor, but don't just ignore increased odors. They could indicate specific problems, such as periodontal disease, impacted anal sacs, seborrhea, ear infections, or even kidney disease. Any strong odor should be checked by your veterinarian.

There is evidence that the immune system may be less effective in older dogs. This means that it is increasingly important to shield your dog from infectious disease, chilling, overheating, and any stressful conditions. Older dogs present a somewhat greater anesthesia risk. Most of this increased risk can be negated, however, by first screening dogs with a complete medical workup.

Long trips may be grueling, and boarding in a kennel may be extremely upsetting. Introduction of a puppy or new pet may be welcomed and may encourage your older dog to play, but if your dog is not used to other dogs, the newcomer will more likely be resented and be an additional source of stress.

The older dog should see its veterinarian at least biyearly, but the owner must take responsibility for observing any health changes. Some of the more common changes, along with some of the more common conditions they may indicate in older dogs, are:
• Limping: arthritis, patellar luxation.
• Nasal discharge: tumor, periodontal disease.
• Coughing: heart disease, tracheal collapse, lung cancer.
• Difficulty eating: periodontal disease, oral tumors.
• Decreased appetite: kidney, liver, or heart disease, pancreatitis, cancer.
• Increased appetite: diabetes, Cushing's syndrome.
• Weight loss: heart, liver, or kidney disease, diabetes, cancer.
• Abdominal distension: heart or kidney disease, Cushing's syndrome, tumor.
• Increased urination: diabetes, kidney or liver disease, cystitis, Cushing's syndrome.
• Diarrhea: kidney or liver disease, pancreatitis.

The above list is by no means inclusive of all symptoms or problems they may indicate. Vomiting and diarrhea can signal many different problems; keep in mind that a small older dog cannot tolerate the dehydration that results from continued vomiting or diarrhea and you should not let it continue unchecked.

In general, any ailment that an older dog has is magnified in severity compared to the same symptoms in a younger dog. The owner of any older dog must be even more careful and

The older Min Pin, though still relatively active, may have a tendency to gain weight.

attentive as his or her dog ages. Don't be lulled into a false sense of security just because you own a miniature pinscher. A long life depends upon good genes, good care, and good luck.

'Til Death Do Us Part

Unfortunately there comes the time when, no matter how diligent you have been, neither you nor your veterinarian can prevent your friend from succumbing to old age or an incurable illness. It seems hard to believe that you will have to say good-bye to someone who has been such a focal point of your life; in truth, a real member of your family. That dogs live such a short time compared to humans is a cruel fact, and as much as you may wish otherwise, your Min Pin is a dog and is not immortal.

You should realize that both of you have been fortunate to have shared so many good times, but make sure that your Min Pin's remaining time is still pleasurable. Many terminal illnesses make your pet feel very bad, and there comes a point where your desire to keep your friend with you as long as possible may not be the kindest thing for either of you. Ask your veterinarian if there is a reasonable chance of your dog getting better, and if it is likely your pet is suffering. Ask yourself if your dog is getting pleasure out of life, and if it enjoys most of its days. If your Min Pin no longer eats its dinner or treats, this is a sign that it does not feel well and you must face the prospect of doing what is best for your beloved friend. Euthanasia is painless and involves giving an overdose of an anesthetic. If your dog is scared of the vet's office, you might feel better having the doctor meet you at home or come out to your car. Although it won't be easy, try to remain with your Min Pin so that its last moments will be filled with your

The older Min Pin especially needs a soft, warm bed.

love; otherwise have a friend that your dog knows stay with your dog. Try to recall the wonderful times you have shared and realize that however painful losing such a once-in-a-lifetime dog is, it is better than never having had such a friend in the first place.

Many people who regarded their pet as a member of the family nonetheless feel embarrassed at the grief they feel at its loss. Yet this dog has often functioned as a surrogate child, best friend, and confidant. Everyone should be lucky enough to find a human with the faithful and loving qualities of their dogs. In some ways, the loss of a pet can be harder than that of more distant family members, especially because the support from friends that comes with human loss is too often absent with pet loss. Such well-meaning but ill-informed statements as "he was just a dog" or "just get another one" do little to ease the pain, but the truth is that many people simply don't know how to react and probably aren't really as callous as they might sound. There are, however, many people who share your feelings and there are pet bereavement counselors available at many veterinary schools.

After losing such a dog, many people say they will never get another. True, no dog will ever take the place of your dog. But you will find that another dog is a welcome diversion and will help keep you from dwelling on the loss of your first pet, as long as you don't keep comparing the new dog to the old. True also, by getting another dog you are sentencing yourself to the same grief in another 10 to 15 years, but wouldn't you rather have that than miss out on all of the love and companionship altogether?

Breeding Min Pins of Merit

Why You *Don't* Want to Breed

One of the most unfortunate aspects of dog ownership is the compulsion so many people have to breed a litter. Rarely is this done with any foresight or responsibility, and the result, most often, is a grave disservice to themselves, their pets, the breed, and the resulting puppies. Unless you have studied the breed, have proven your female to be a superior specimen in terms of conformation, health, and temperament, and plan to take responsibility for each and every puppy for the rest of its life, you have no business doing anything but having your dog neutered. Keep in mind:

• A litter is extremely expensive! Stud fee, prenatal care, whelping complications, cesarean sections, supplemental feeding, puppy food, vaccinations, advertising, and a staggering investment of time and energy are all involved.

• There is definite discomfort and a certain amount of danger to any dog, but especially a very small dog, when whelping a litter. Watching a litter be born is not a good way to teach the children the miracle of life; there are too many things that can go very wrong.

• A spayed female is far less likely to develop breast cancer and a number of other hormone-related diseases. She should be spayed before her first season in order to avoid these problems.

• Serious breeders have spent years researching genetics and the breed; they breed only the best specimens, and screen for hereditary defects in order to obtain superior puppies. Until you have done the same, you are undoing the hard work of those who have dedicated their lives to bettering the breed.

• Finding responsible buyers is very, very difficult, and you may find yourself at wit's end caring for a houseful of Min Pin juvenile delinquents. You may find homes, but will they really be good homes?

• There are many more purebred miniature pinschers in the world than there are good homes for them. The puppy you sell to a less-than-perfect buyer may end up neglected or discarded, or used to produce puppies to sell to even less desirable homes. Millions of purebreds are euthanized each year at pounds. Sometimes they are the lucky ones.

• The fact that your Min Pin is purebred and registered does not mean it is breeding quality, any more than the fact that you have a driver's license qualifies you to build race cars. Everybody thinks his or her own dog is special, and it is. But that doesn't mean it should be bred. (See All Min Pins Are Not Created Equal, page 13.)

• You will be unpleasantly surprised at the number of friends who just "had to have one of Greta's pups" who will suddenly disappear from your life, develop allergies, or otherwise opt out of taking a puppy when the time comes.

Cute as buttons, but what kind of homes will they find?

Ethical breeders breed a litter only after studying the breed standard, pedigrees, and individual dogs to find the most advantageous match of conformation, temperament, and health. Then, after proving the worth of both prospective parents through competitions, they interview prospective buyers and get deposits from them before the breeding even takes place. They have money set aside for prenatal and postnatal care, and emergency funds and vacation time available for whelping or postwhelping complications. They have the commitment to keep every single puppy born for the rest of its life should good homes not be available or should they ever have to be returned. And they worry a lot. Is it any wonder that some of the best breeders breed the least?

Breeding the Right Way

If you still have not been dissuaded from breeding your Min Pin, you owe it to yourself and the breed to settle for no less than the best available miniature pinscher stud. You will not find this stud advertised in the newspaper,

nor living down the street. If you are contemplating breeding, it is assumed that you have now learned enough about the breed that you are familiar with prominent kennels and studs, and you know the good and bad points of your own female. Look for a stud that is superior in the areas in which your female needs improvement. Look for a stud owner who is honest about his or her dog's faults, health problems, and temperament. You want someone who is trustworthy, dependable, and experienced in breeding. A responsible stud owner will have proven the stud by earning titles, will have complete records and photos of other litters the stud has produced, and will insist that your bitch and her pedigree be compatible, and your facilities adequate, before accepting her for breeding.

Min Pin Kin

Once you have narrowed your list to several potential studs, you will want to consider their pedigrees. The pedigree is more than just a list of strange names that you can trot out to impress your friends. It is a history of breeding decisions that outlines the genetic heritage of each dog. Careful breeders search out pictures and descriptions of the dogs in their pedigrees (most champion dogs have pictures available in Min Pin magazines and breed history books); in this way they are able to predict how puppies from a contemplated union will turn out.

The pedigree can also tell you how closely related the prospective sire and dam are. *Inbreeding* refers to a system of mating that makes it more likely that an offspring will inherit identical copies of the same gene from both its mother and father. The problem with inbreeding lies in the fact that the majority of serious hereditary defects are recessive in nature, meaning that two identical copies of the gene for that defect must be inherited for the trait to be expressed—exactly what inbreeding promotes! Unless there is a specific reason to inbreed, and you have a firm grasp of the genetic principles involved, and are intimately familiar with the dogs in the pedigree, such close breeding is not advisable.

A breeding with a concerted effort to intensify the genetic influence of a particular individual is called a *line-breeding*; in it one name will appear over and over. Such a breeding will also be somewhat inbred, and carries the same caveat (though usually to a lesser degree) as does inbreeding.

If there are no common names in the pedigree, then the breeding is an *outcross*. This is generally the safest way to go, but has the shortcoming that the results are less predictable.

Genetics of the Miniature Pinscher

Dogs have 78 pairs of chromosomes, each containing many genes (sequences of DNA that direct cells to develop in certain ways). In each pair there are two sets of alternate genes, known as alleles: one inherited from the sire, the other from the dam. If the two alleles are not alike, one allele (the dominant one) may mask the presence of the other (recessive) one.

Not all traits are passed in this simple "dominant/recessive" nature. Many are the result of many pairs of alleles all working together to produce subtle degrees of variation. Size is an example of such "polygenic" inheritance; a large Min Pin bred to a small one would more likely have offspring intermediate in size, although there would be considerable variation in what size the offspring actually would be. There are still many traits for which the genetic aspects are not yet understood; when in doubt, the best thing to do is to avoid breeding dogs with similar faults.

Health and Heredity

Most traits, whether physical or behavioral, are influenced both by genetic and environmental aspects. Because the hereditary aspects of many health and temperament problems are not always understood, it is best to take a cautious approach when contemplating breeding. Both Legg-Perthes disease and PRA are thought to be recessively inherited, undescended testicles and patellar luxation are thought to be due to the interaction of many genes, and demodectic mange tends to be passed from dams to offspring though the genetics involved are not understood. There are too many wonderful healthy miniature pinschers available that can produce wonderful, healthy puppies; why take a chance with a less-than-healthy dam?

Min Pin Prenuptials

Long before your female comes into season, you should have a written contract with the stud dog owner that spells out what fees will be due and when, and what will happen if only one or no puppies are born. Both dogs to be bred should have a blood test for canine brucellosis, a primarily (but not exclusively) sexually transmitted disease with devastating effects on fertility. The female should also have a prebreeding checkup to ensure that she is in good health, has current vaccinations, and does not have any abnormalities that would make whelping difficult.

Monitor the female closely for signs of "heat" (estrus). These include swelling of the vulva and a red discharge, but in many Min Pins these signs may be subtle and go unnoticed. Most dogs are breedable for several days sometime between the eighth and eighteenth day of estrus, although earlier and later alliances have been known to result in pregnancy. Your

Predicting Coat Color

Min Pins can vary in both their pattern of coloration or in their shade of coloring, and several different genes are involved in determining what the final product will be. The genetics are not as clear-cut as in some breeds, but the following model works in most cases:

Min Pins come in two basic patterns: self-colored—meaning basically the same color all over—such as red or stag red, and tan-pointed, as in the black and tan. These are controlled by genes at the **A**-locus:

• A^s: Self-colored; dominant, so that self-colored dogs can have either the gene pair A^s/A^s or A^s/a^t.

• a^t: Tan-pointed; recessive, so that tan-pointed dogs must have the gene pair a^t/a^t.

The above is the typical way these genes act in most breeds, but the situation is not so clear-cut in Min Pins. For example, there are reports that two red dogs bred together can produce both reds and black and tans, and two black and tans bred together can produce both reds and black and tans. This is probably because of the additional interaction with the genes at another location, the **E** genes. These genes also determine whether a dog is red or stag red.

• **E**: Allows black hairs to form. A stag red (or a black and tan) needs at least one copy of **E** (**E/E** or **E/e**).

• **e**: Does not allow black hair to form. Clear reds must have two copies (**e/e**).

This means that stag red, clear red, and tan pointed dogs can be produced from all combinations of parental colors with the following exceptions:

• Clear red bred to clear red should only result in clear red offspring.

• Tan-pointed bred to tan-pointed should result in only tan-pointed and clear red offspring.

A tan-pointed dog can be black and tan, chocolate and tan, or blue and tan. These colors are controlled by genes at two other locations:

Gray versus black is determined by the **D** gene:

• **D**: Causes any black hair to be intensely pigmented, or black. Dominant, so that dogs with black hairs can be either **D/D** or **D/d**.

• **d**: Causes any black hair to be diluted, or grayish. The resultant color is called "blue." Recessive, so that any blue dogs are **d/d**.

Brown versus black is determined by the **B** gene:

• **B**: Causes any black hair to be black. Dominant, so that dogs with black hairs can be either **B/B** or **B/b**.

• **b**: Causes any black hair to be brown, liver, or "chocolate." Recessive, so that any chocolate dogs are **b/b**. Such dogs also have brown, rather than black, noses, and light-colored eyes.

The fun starts when you begin to predict colors while keeping in mind the interactions between the patterns and colors. What happens if a dog has the genotype a^t/a^t **E/E d/d b/b**? All of the areas that are usually black will be diluted by both **b** and **d**, and the result will be a fawn individual, the color referred to in Doberman pinschers as "Isabella." This color is virtually unseen in Min Pins, because the **b** gene is rare and the **d** gene is rarer, but it is possible.

veterinarian can also monitor your female Min Pin's progress with vaginal smears or blood tests. As she approaches her receptive stage, she will tend to "flag" her tail, or cock it to the side when the male approaches or if you scratch around the base of her tail. Your best indicator is the stud dog; experienced stud dogs do not need calendars or microscopes!

Breeding dogs involves more than just letting a male and female loose together. Although this may seem like the natural way, in fact it is not natural for two dogs to breed when they may have just met each other. Neither dog knows the other well enough to trust its actions, so the female will often snap in fear when the male mounts, and the male may be dissuaded from mounting by her actions. Instead, after an initial period for introductions and flirting, the female should be held for the male. This is more easily accomplished if both dogs are put on a table (preferably against the wall in a corner, and on a rubber bath mat). If the male is smaller than the female, as is often the case with Min Pins, he may not be able to reach unless you provide him with a book on which to stand. With a reluctant female, the owner can support her under her hind legs with one hand; she can also be guided toward a male that might have bad aim, because attempts to guide the male will usually discourage him. Upon intromission the male will step from side to side, and then will want to jump off of the female and turn by lifting one hind leg over her back, so that they can stand rear to rear. This "tie" is perfectly normal for dogs and will typically last from 10 to 30 minutes. Keep both of them cool and calm during this time. Min Pins are very capable breeders and usually need very little assistance from humans.

For optimal chances of conception, repeat the breeding every other day

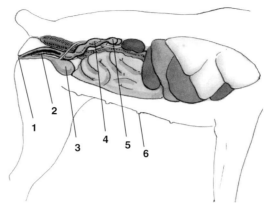

Reproductive organs of the female:

1. *Vulva*
2. *Vagina*
3. *Bladder*
4. *Developing embryo*
5. *Ovary*
6. *Teat*

until the female will no longer accept the male. Be sure to keep her away from other males during this time; dogs are not known for their fidelity! The AKC will not recognize litters fathered by more than one sire.

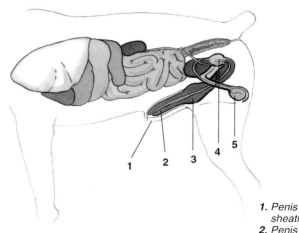

Reproductive organs of the male:

1. *Penis sheath*
2. *Penis*
3. *Bulb*
4. *Prostate*
5. *Testes*

71

Min Pin Pregnancy

Now you have two months to wait and plan. Gradually increase and change the expectant mother's food to a high-quality puppy food as time progresses. Keep her in shape, because a well-conditioned dog will have fewer problems whelping. At the end of the first month, your veterinarian may be able to feel the developing puppies, but this is not always accurate. Two encouraging signs of pregnancy that will appear at around this same time are a clear mucous discharge from the vagina and enlarged, pink nipples. If at any time the discharge is not clear, seek veterinary attention at once.

After the first month, avoid letting your pregnant Min Pin jump from high places. When carrying her, be sure that you are not putting pressure on her abdomen. Do not give any medication without your veterinarian's advice. Your pregnant female should be isolated from strange dogs beginning

Preparing for Delivery

The whelping kit should include:
- A whelping box.
- A rectal thermometer.
- Many towels and washcloths.
- A nasal aspirator.
- Dull, blunt-nosed scissors.
- Dental floss.
- A heating pad or heat lamp.
- A warm box for placing newborns in while awaiting the arrival of any siblings.
- Bitch's milk replacement.
- Highlighted whelping instructions.
- Emergency phone numbers.

three weeks before her due date; exposure to certain viruses during that time does not allow her to develop sufficient immunity to pass to her puppies, and can result in the loss of the litter.

Many females are prone to false pregnancies: a condition in which the breasts become slightly enlarged and may even have some milk. Pronounced cases involving large amounts of milk production, weight gain, and even nesting behavior and the adoption of certain toys as "babies" may be unhealthy and should be checked by your veterinarian. Some can be so convincing that even experienced breeders have thought their bitch was in whelp until she failed to deliver puppies!

The Delivery Room

If you have never assisted at a small dog whelping, talk to your veterinarian or an experienced Min Pin breeder about what to expect. Arrange to have someone on call in case of any difficulty.

You should prepare a whelping box that will double as a nursery, and place it in a warm, quiet room. You can use the bottom of a plastic dog cage, a large cat litter pan, or a sturdy

*Both dogs are tan pointed but the adult shows the influence of the recessive **d** gene, which causes black hair to be gray.*

clean cardboard box. The sides should be high enough so that the young pups cannot get out, but low enough so that the mother can get over without scraping her hanging nipples. You will find it much easier to assist her during whelping if you place the box on a tabletop, but when you cannot monitor her comings and goings you must place it on the floor. Place the box on a rug or over insulating material, and line the inside with newspaper (preferably blank newsprint, but never colored sections), or even better, washable blankets. Don't use indoor-outdoor carpeting, which tends to interact with urine in such a way as to irritate pups' skin.

Special Deliveries

You should be counting the days from the first breeding carefully. Although 63 days is the average canine gestation time, there is some variability, with small dogs tending to be somewhat early rather than late. You can get about 12 hours of advance notice by charting the expectant mother's temperature starting around the fifty-sixth day; when her temperature drops to about 98°F (36.7°C) and remains there, make plans to stay home because labor should begin within 12 hours. Warm the whelping box to 80°F (26.7°C), and prepare for a long night. She will become more restless, refuse to eat, and repeatedly demand to go out. Make her as comfortable as possible and do not let her go outside alone where she might have a puppy.

The birth of puppies is extremely messy, so at this point you should remove any blankets you wish to save. As labor becomes more intense, she may scratch and bite at her bedding. The puppies are preceded by a water bag; once this has burst, the first puppy should be born soon. As each baby is born, help the mother

clear its face so it can breathe; then you may wish to tie off the umbilical cord about 0.75 inch (1.9 cm) from the puppy with dental floss, and then cut it on the side away from the pup. If you prefer, you can let the mother cut the cord, but watch to make sure she doesn't injure the pup. Her chewing action crushes the cord and prevents it from bleeding. Each puppy should be followed by an afterbirth, which the dam will try to eat. Allow her to eat one, as they contain important hormones affecting milk production, but eating too many will give her diarrhea. You must count the placentas to make absolutely sure that none was retained in her; retained placentas can cause serious infection. Dry the puppy and place it on the mother's nipple to nurse. You may have to help it by opening its mouth and squeezing a bit of milk into it. When the dam begins to strain to produce the next puppy, remove the first one to your other temporary box warmed to 90°F (32.2°C).

The nursing dam must be watched carefully for signs of mastitis.

When to Call the Veterinarian

You may have a whelping emergency if:

• More than 24 hours have passed since her temperature dropped without the onset of contractions.

• More than two hours of intermittent contractions have passed without progressing to hard, forceful contractions.

• More than 30 minutes have passed of strong contractions without producing a puppy.

• More than 15 minutes have passed since part of a puppy protruded through the vulva and the puppy makes no progress.

• Large amounts of blood are passed during whelping. The normal color fluid is dark green to black.

Never allow a dam in trouble to continue unaided. She may need a cesarean section to save her life, and the longer it is put off the poorer the chances of survival for her and her puppies will be.

Min Pin Mommas

It is not always easy to tell when the last baby is born. If you have any doubts, have your veterinarian check the dam (you should bring her and the

An ideal whelping box has a rail around the side so that pups cannot be accidentally caught between the dam and the side.

puppies for a post-birth check the next day anyway). It is normal for the dam to have a dark bloody vaginal discharge for a week or two after the birth, but any signs of infection or foul odor associated with it is cause for immediate concern.

Sometimes the dam's breasts become hard, swollen, or painful, indicating mastitis. Warm compresses can help her feel more comfortable, but if pus and blood are mixed with the milk, you will need to prevent the pups from nursing from those nipples and your veterinarian will probably prescribe antibiotics.

Eclampsia is a life-threatening convulsive condition that may occur in late pregnancy or, more commonly, during lactation. It is more prevalent in small breeds and with large litters. The first signs are nervous panting, followed by vomiting and disorientation. Increasing muscular twitching and body temperature are definite danger signals. Convulsions are the last stage before death.

The condition seems to be brought about by a depletion of calcium. Many breeders of small dogs used to supplement with calcium throughout the pregnancy in an attempt to ward off eclampsia, but it is now thought that such supplementation may actually promote eclampsia by interfering with the internal calcium-regulating mechanisms.

Once eclampsia does occur, the bitch must be taken immediately to the veterinarian for an injection of calcium and vitamin D in order to save her life. You may try giving calcium by mouth if she can swallow and if the trip to the veterinarian is long. *This is an emergency.*

In cases of infections, mastitis, or eclampsia, you may have to wean the puppies early. By fitting the mother with a "body suit," such as a sock or sweater sleeve with four leg holes, she can stay with the pups without letting them nurse.

Min Pin Puppies

Monitor the nursing puppies to make sure they are getting milk. Pups with cleft palates will have milk bubbling out of their nostrils as they attempt to nurse. Some pups must be helped onto the dam's nipples; some dams have nipples that are too large to fit in a pup's mouth. You should weigh each puppy daily on a gram scale to make sure that it is gaining weight. If not, ask your veterinarian about supplemental feeding.

Puppies cannot regulate their body temperature, and chilling can quickly result in death. This is especially critical for small breeds. The dam is understandably reluctant to leave them at first; you should place them in a warm box and encourage the dam to go out to the elimination site on a regular schedule. Use a heat lamp or heating pad to maintain the pups' environment at 85 to 90°F (29.4–32.2°C) for the first week, 80°F (26.7°C) for the second week, and 75°F (23.9°C) for the third and fourth weeks. Never feed a chilled puppy, except for a few drops of sugar water.

Min Pin puppies are born with pink noses and eye rims that gradually turn dark beginning a few days after birth. Colors may change with maturation. Reds and rust markings tend to become richer, and small white chest spots or very small thumb marks will often disappear by maturity.

The puppies' eyes will open starting at around ten days of age, and their ears at around two weeks. This age marks the beginning of rapid mental and physical growth. They will attempt to walk at two weeks of age. Be sure to give them solid footing (*not* slippery newspaper!).

The dam will usually begin to wean her pups by four to six weeks of age;

smaller pups may need to stay with her longer. At around three weeks, you can introduce the puppies to food: baby food or baby cereal or dry dog food mixed with water and put through the blender is a good starter. They may lick it off your finger or you may have to put their noses in it. No matter what technique you use, be prepared to declare the feeding arena a major disaster area by the time the meal is over. Puppies seem to think they can best eat with their feet!

Docking and Cropping

Tails should be docked, and dewclaws removed, at approximately three days of age. Your veterinarian, or a very experienced breeder, can do this. Cropping, however, must only be done by a veterinarian, and is not performed until 12 weeks of age. A veterinarian with considerable experience cropping Min Pin ears is best; dogs with floppy ears will require a shorter crop in order to make sure they will stand erect. Cropping requires both surgical expertise and an artistic eye; both are essential for the perfect ears.

Even the best cropping will prove unsatisfactory if the ears are not subsequently attended to. This will require cleaning and taping for several weeks. An experienced veterinarian or breeder should guide you through this process.

A Good Home for Life

After about six weeks of age, it is important that the puppies meet people so that they are well socialized, but this does not mean that they need to be exposed to a constant stream of new faces. Young puppies are irresistible, and your house may become the newest tourist attraction on the block. Don't let the puppies be overhandled, and don't allow the mother to become stressed by onlookers. Talk to your veterinarian about your puppies' vaccination schedule and visitors, who

Supplemental feeding may be necessary.

This proud mother and her offspring will depend upon the breeder to place the pups in only the best of homes.

could bring contagious diseases with them.

Because the miniature pinscher puppy has little weight to spare, any undue stress or small illness could have serious consequences. An underweight puppy is best kept at home until it has built up some reserves, especially if being placed in an inexperienced home.

There are two ways to place puppies—the ethical way and the unethical way. The unethical way is easy: Place an ad in the paper or by the road, sell each pup to the first comer for whatever you can get, and as soon as it leaves your house wipe your hands of it. Don't think about the new owner who may not have a clue about raising a dog, who may think a Min Pin will be a fine outdoor watchdog,

or who is simply desperate for a Christmas present for the kids but really has no desire to keep it past the time they tire of it, or who wants a little moneymaker that will be a puppy machine living in a cage until it dies of neglect. Yes, the unethical way is easy, until you try to sleep at night, every night for the next 12 years or so as you lay awake wondering what fate you sealed for the little being who trusted you to care about its future.

The ethical way is initially more difficult, but will be easier if you have quality puppies with which to attract quality homes. If you have a quality breeding, word of mouth within the Min Pin world and at dog shows will be your best advertisement, but you can supplement with ads in dog magazines, and in various newspapers. You must play detective in ascertaining if prospective buyers have the sort of home in which you would be comfortable placing a puppy. One breeder relates that she evaluates prospective buyers by whether, if she had to give up the mother dog, she could be confident that this person would provide a good home for her. Once a sale has been made, the ethical breeder maintains contact with the puppy owner; and finally, the ethical breeder agrees that no matter what the age and what the reason, that if the new owner can no longer keep the dog, it is always welcome back at its birthplace. If you can't make the commitment to be an ethical breeder, it is best not to be a breeder at all.

It may take time, but you can find a good home. Of course, after a while it may become obvious that good home you find is your own!

Min Pin Trials and Tribulations

Many Min Pin owners are understandably proud of their pets, and most Min Pins are exceedingly proud of themselves. The world of dogs provides many opportunities for proud owners and Min Pins to show off their mental and physical attributes. If you plan to breed your Min Pin, you should plan to compete in conformation in order to demonstrate to others that your dog is as perfect as you know it is. But even for the Min Pin that is less than a physical Adonis, there are plenty of ways to shine.

Min Pin Mind Power

Your gifted Min Pin can earn degrees attesting to its mastery of various levels of obedience. You and your dog will have to prove yourselves in front of a judge at three different obedience trials in order to officially have an obedience title become part of your dog's name.

The most elementary degree, Companion Dog (CD), requires mostly the same commands that you should plan to teach your dog anyway for use around the home: Heel, Sit, Down, Come, and Stay. The only added requirement is the "stand for exam," in which your pet stands still, off-lead and with you 6 feet (1.8 m) away while the judge approaches and touches the dog. This is also a useful exercise in everyday life, for example, at the veterinarian's. If this all sounds too easy for your little genius, don't worry: more advanced degrees of Companion Dog Excellent (CDX) or Utility Dog (UD) also require retrieving, jumping, hand signals, and scent discrimination. The AKC will send you a free pamphlet describing obedience trial regulations.

The best preparation for obedience trials can be found at obedience classes conducted by obedience trial competitors. As a small dog owner, you must always exercise more caution than the average dog owner. Let other members of your obedience class know that your dog could be injured by theirs if they do not keep theirs under control. At the same time,

Advanced obedience degrees require the retrieval of a dumbbell, such as the one shown here. Note that blue Min Pins, though disqualified from conformation competition, are welcome to compete in obedience.

keep your Min Pin under control so that it does not start a fracas, or even scare the big dogs.

If you enter competition with your Min Pin, remember this as your golden rule: Companion Dog means just that; being upset at your dog because it made a mistake defeats the purpose of obedience as a way of promoting a harmonious partnership between trainer and dog. Failing a trial, in the scope of life, is an insignificant event. Never let a ribbon or a few points become more important than a trusting relationship with your companion. Your Min Pin's love for you is unconditional and will not be affected by whether or not you win ribbons. Besides, chances are you'll make as many errors as your Min Pin, and you can be sure your Min Pin will forgive you!

Min Pin Man Trailers

The dog's sense of smell is one of its most awe-inspiring attributes. Although one never sees a pack of Min Pins hot on the trail of the escaped prisoner in the movies, nonetheless Min Pins have an acute sense of smell and are quite capable of following a trail. One training method is to drop tidbits every few feet along a trail laid by the owner (or other tracklayer), and encourage the dog to find them. The dog gradually learns that by following the trail it will come across hidden treasures. Eventually fewer and fewer treats are used, but there is the mother lode of dog biscuits awaiting at the end of the trail. If you would like to test the waters, you can evaluate your Min Pin's propensity to use its nose by hiding dog biscuits around the house or yard and then having your dog sniff them out. Tracking aficionados are perhaps the most devoted of dog trainers, and enjoy the solitude of spending the morning alone with their special dog. Dogs that pass an AKC-

sanctioned test are awarded the titles Tracking Dog (TD) and Tracking Dog Excellent (TDX).

The Nimble Min Pin

If any breed defines agility, it is the miniature pinscher! In organized agility competition, dogs must negotiate a course of obstacles and jumps, including an A-frame, seesaw, elevated board walk, tunnels, and a variety of high and broad jumps (adjusted according to the height of the dog). There are Novice, Open, and Excellent classes, and the AKC awards, in increasing level of difficulty, the titles Novice Agility Dog (NAD), Open Agility Dog (OAD), Agility Dog Excellent (ADE), and Master Agility Excellent (MAX). Agility combines obedience, athleticism, and quickness; sound like any breed you know?

The Min Pin Pinup

A quirk of human nature leads many dog owners to assert that "my dog's better than your dog"; some people try to prove it at dog shows. Here the Min Pins come into the show ring to strut their stuff and pose for all to admire. The judge examines each one from head to tail and ranks them in accordance to their adherence to the official breed standard. But it's more than just a beauty contest. Each dog's bone structure and movement are evaluated for soundness and the absence of lameness or deformities. If you find yourself admiring your dog as its struts and poses around the yard, you may be interested in showing it off at a conformation show. The best place to start is by getting an honest opinion from your dog's breeder. As long as your Min Pin has no disqualifying faults, you can show it; of course, you may not win, but you will still learn a lot about the show world and be better prepared in the event that you would like to show your next miniature pinscher.

Assuming that you want to take the plunge, you will need to train your Min Pin to pose and trot. If you go to a dog show, the first thing you will notice is that Min Pins are not shown in the same constrained manner as are most breeds. Unlike other breeds, much of the judging of Min Pins is done while the Min Pin intermittently poses and reposes itself without the overt aid of its handler. However, for the judge to evaluate your dog closely, the handler will need to pose it on a tabletop in the ring, placing its legs by hand to best show off its conformation. The correct Min Pin show pose is with all four paws pointing straight forward, legs parallel to each other and per-pendicular to the ground, tail held up (either naturally or by the handler) at about a 45-degree angle, and head and ears up. If your dog already knows the stand for exam, you have a head start. Reward the dog for keep-ing its feet where you place them, and for looking alert. Most handlers use a small squeaky toy or boiled liver to get the dog's attention in the ring. Besides looking good standing still, your Min Pin will need to look good at a trot. The correct trot is done in a dead straight line, with the dog's head and tail held naturally high, and at a speed that accentuates the hackney gait. The Min Pin that is brimming with con-fidence can show itself off and is at a great advantage in the show ring. But don't expect instant self-confidence without first practicing around other dogs and people. There are profes-sional handlers who will show your dog for you and probably win more often than you would; however, there is nothing like the thrill of winning when you are on the other end of the lead! That lead, incidentally, is a spe-cial very thin show lead, available from dog show vendors.

Contact your local kennel or even obedience club to find out if either has

The miniature pinscher is a show dog par excellence.

handling classes, or when the next match will be held. Matches are infor-mal events where everybody is learn-ing: puppies, handlers, even the judges. Win or lose, never take one judge's opinion too seriously, and no matter how obviously feebleminded the judge is, be polite and keep your comments to yourself.

At a real AKC show, each time a judge chooses your dog as the best dog of its sex that is not already a Champion, it wins up to 5 points, depending upon how many dogs it defeats. To become an AKC Champion (CH), your Min Pin must win 15 points including two majors (defeating enough dogs to win 3 to 5 points at a time). You may enter any class for which your dog is eligible: Puppy, Novice, American Bred, Bred by Exhibitor, or Open. The Best of Breed classes are for dogs that are already Champions. Before entering, you should contact the AKC and ask for the rules and regulations con-cerning dog shows, which will explain the requirements for each class. Your dog must be entered

"When I grow up I'm going to be a big star!" No matter what your Min Pin does, its most important starring role is in that of family member.

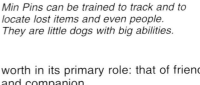

Min Pins can be trained to track and to locate lost items and even people. They are little dogs with big abilities.

about three weeks before the show date, and you will need to get a premium list and entry form from the appropriate show superintendent (their addresses are available from the AKC or most dog magazines).

To survive as a conformation competitor, you must be able to separate your own ego and self-esteem from your dog; many people cannot do this. You must also not allow your dog's ability to win in the ring cloud your perception of your dog's true worth in its primary role: that of friend and companion.

Your Min Pin never has to step foot in a show ring, earn a title, or thrill anyone except you to be the champion of your heart. Whatever you consider to be fun, your little friend will agree with. Whether sitting beside you watching TV, sneaking a snack under the table, or patrolling the neighborhood on-lead, your miniature pinscher will be delighted because it is doing it with its best friend: you.

The show dog must know how to pose on a table, aided by its handler who may place its feet and hold its head and tail.

The Min Pin Blueprint

What makes a champion? In the show ring, it is the adherence to a very exacting blueprint of the ideal Min Pin, known as the breed standard of perfection. No one dog ever fits that blueprint perfectly, but at the very least a dog should fit it well enough so that it is easily recognized as a miniature pinscher. This possession of breed attributes is known as type, and is an important requirement of any purebred. A dog should also be built in such a way that it can go about its daily life with minimal exertion and absence of lameness. This equally important attribute is known as soundness. Add to these the attributes of good health and temperament, and you have the four cornerstones of the ideal miniature pinscher.

Min Pin Nomenclature

• Short-coupled: A comparatively short loin.
• Foreface: The muzzle.
• Scissors bite: A bite in which the outer sides of the bottom incisors touch the inner side of the top incisors.
• Self-colored: Of the same color as the surrounding coat.
• Dewlap: Pendulous loose skin under the neck.
• Throatiness: Excessive loose skin under the throat.
• Well-sprung ribs: A somewhat rounded rib cage.
• Loin: The area between the ribs and the hindquarters.
• Croup: The upper region of the pelvis, delimited by the hipbones and the point of the buttocks.
• Shoulders clean and sloping: Shoulder blades set obliquely, with the highest point not disrupting a flowing line from the neck into the topline.
• Dewclaws: An extra toe on the inside of the leg.
• Catlike feet: Round, compact feet.
• Closely knit toes: Toes are close together.
• Well-angulated: Usually refers to a series of 90-degree angles between the pelvis, knee, and hock in the hindquarters, and between the withers, shoulder/upper arm joint, and elbow in the forequarters.
• Stifle: The dog's "knee."
• Vent region: Area around the anus.

The stylish high stepping hackney gait is an important and distinctive trait of the miniature pinscher.

The AKC Miniature Pinscher Standard

General appearance: The miniature pinscher is structurally a well-balanced, sturdy, compact, short-coupled, smooth-coated dog. It naturally is well-groomed, proud, vigorous, and alert. Characteristic traits are its hackneylike action, fearless animation, complete self-possession, and spirited presence.

Size, proportion, substance: *Size:* 10 to 12.5 inches (25.4–31.8 cm) in height allowed, with desired height 11 to 11.5 inches (27.9–29.2 cm) measured at the highest point of the shoulder blades. *Disqualification:* Under 10 inches (25.4 cm) or over 12.5 inches (31.8 cm) in height. Length of males equals height at the withers. Females may be slightly longer.

Head: In correct proportion to the body. Tapering, narrow with well-fitted but not too prominent foreface that balances well with the skull. No indication of coarseness. Eyes full, slightly oval, clear, bright, and dark even to a true black, including eye rims with the exception of chocolates, whose eye rims should be self-colored. Ears are set high, standing erect from the base to the tip. May be cropped or uncropped. The skull appears flat, tapering toward the muzzle. The muzzle is strong rather than fine and delicate, and in proportion to the head as a whole. The head is well-balanced with only a slight drop to the muzzle, which is parallel to the top of the skull. The nose is black only, with the exception of chocolates, which should have a self-colored nose. The lips and cheeks are small, taut, and closely adherent to each other. The teeth meet in a scissors bite.

Neck, topline, body: *Neck:* Proportioned to the head and the body, slightly arched, gracefully curved, blending into the shoulders, muscular and free from suggestion of

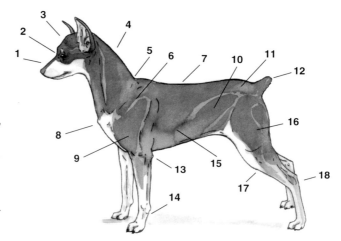

The external anatomy of the miniature pinscher.

dewlap or throatiness. *Topline:* Back level or slightly sloping toward the rear both when standing and gaiting. *Body:* Compact, slightly wedgeshaped, and muscular. The forechest is well-developed, with well-sprung ribs. Depth of brisket, the baseline of which is level with points of the elbows. The belly is moderately tucked up to denote grace of structural form. Short and strong in loin. The croup should be level with the topline. The tail is set high, held erect, and docked in proportion to the size of the dog.

Forequarters: *Shoulders:* Clean and sloping with moderate angulation coordinated to permit the hackneylike action. Elbows should be close to the body. *Legs:* Strong bone development and small clean joints. As viewed from the front, straight and upstanding. Pasterns should be strong, perpendicular. Dewclaws should be removed. *Feet:* Small, catlike, toes strong, well-arched, and closely knit with deep pads. Nails should be thick and blunt.

Hindquarters: Well-muscled quarters set wide enough apart to fit into a

1. Foreface or muzzle
2. Stop
3. Skull
4. Neckline
5. Withers
6. Shoulder
7. Back
8. Forechest
9. Upper arm
10. Loin
11. Croup
12. Tail
13. Elbow
14. Pastern
15. Rib cage
16. Thigh
17. Knee
18. Hock

A good visualization of the standard.

properly balanced body. As viewed from the rear, the legs are straight and parallel. From the side, well angulated. The thighs are well muscled. The stifles are well-defined. The hocks are short, set well apart. Dewclaws should be removed. The feet are small, catlike, toes strong, well-arched, and closely knit with deep pads. The nails should be thick and blunt.

Coat: Smooth, hard, and short, straight and lustrous, closely adhering to and uniformly covering the body.

Color: Solid clear red. Stag red (red with intermingling of black hairs). Black with sharply defined rust-red markings on cheeks, lips, lower jaw, throat, twin spots above eyes and chest, lower half of forelegs, inside of hind legs and vent region, lower portion of hocks and feet. Black pencil stripes on toes. Chocolate with rust-red markings the same as specified for blacks, except brown pencil stripes on toes. In the solid red and stag red a rich, vibrant medium to dark shade is preferred. *Disqualification:* Any color other than listed. Thumb mark (patch of black hair surrounded by rust on the front of the foreleg between the foot and the wrist; on chocolates, the patch is chocolate hair). White on any part of the dog that exceeds 0.5 inch (1.3 cm) in its longest dimension.

Gait: The forelegs and hind legs move parallel, with feet turning neither in nor out. The hackneylike action is a high-stepping, reaching, free and easy gait in which the front leg moves straight forward and in front of the body and the foot bends at the wrist. The dog drives smoothly and strongly from the rear. The head and tail are carried high.

Temperament: Fearless animation, complete self-possession, and spirited presence.

Disqualifications: Under 10 inches (25.4 cm) or over 12.5 inches (31.8 cm) in height. Any color other than listed. Thumb mark (patch of black hair surrounded by rust on the front of the foreleg between the foot and the wrist; on chocolates, the patch is chocolate hair). White on any part of the dog that exceeds 0.5 inch (1.3 cm) in its longest dimension.

The proper Min Pin head is elegant yet powerful.

Useful Addresses and Literature

Clubs

American Boarding Kennel
  Association
4575 Galley Road, Suite 400A
Colorado Springs, Colorado
  80915

American Kennel Club
51 Madison Avenue
New York, New York 10038
212-696-8200

Miniature Pinscher Club of
  America, Inc.*
Ms. Vivian Hogan, Secretary
26915 Clarksburg Road
Damascus, Maryland 20872

Rescue Coordinator:
Joyce Somero
(810) 656-4132

Orthopedic Foundation for
  Animals
2300 Nifong Boulevard
Columbia, Missouri 65201
(314) 442-0418

Home Again Microchip System
  1-800-LONELY ONE

Books

Boshell, Buris R. *Your Miniature
  Pinscher*. Fairfax, Virginia:
  Denlingers, 1969.

Gaines TWT
P.O. Box 8172
Kankakee, Illinois 60901

Krogh, David. *The King of Toys
  Champion Book*. Gresham,
  Oregon: Garvin Lazertype.

Tietjen, Sari Brewster. *The New
  Miniature Pinscher*. New
  York: Howell Book House,
  MacMillan Publishing, 1988.

Magazines

Dog World
29 North Wacker Drive
Chicago, Illinois 60606-3298
(312) 726-2802

Dog Fancy
P.O. Box 53264
Boulder, Colorado 80322-3264
(303) 666-8504

Dogs USA Annual
P.O. Box 55811
Boulder, Colorado 80322-5811
(303) 786-7652

TNT Toys
8848 Beverly Hills
Lakeland, Florida 33809-1604

Pinscher Patter (available only
  to members of Miniature
  Pinscher Club of America).

Video

Miniature Pinscher #VVT508
The American Kennel Club
Attn: Video Fulfillment
5580 Centerview Drive
Suite 200
Raleigh, North Carolina 27606
919-233-9780

---

* This address may change with the
  election of new club officers. Contact
  the AKC for the current listing, as well
  as for the contacts for local Min Pin
  clubs in your area and the Min Pin
  rescue organization.

Index

The Good-Day Bunnies

SHOPPING DAY

By Harriet Margolin and Carol Nicklaus

A GOLDEN BOOK • NEW YORK
Western Publishing Company, Inc., Racine, Wisconsin 53404

"Does anyone want to come with me to the village?"
Mama asked.

"I do," said Bumper.

"I do," said Becky, his twin sister.

"Me too," said Baby Bonnie.

"Good! Let's go," said Mama. "We have lots of errands
to do."

Mama parked the car in the lot near the train station.
Becky and Bumper jumped out of the car.
"Don't run off without me!" Mama reminded them.

Mama helped everyone across Main Street. Their first stop
was the pharmacy.

"Good day," Mama said to the druggist.

"Good day," he answered. "How can I help you?"

"I'll have a bottle of children's vitamins and a tube of
Triple Ripple toothpaste."

"Can I have this?" Bumper asked, holding up a bottle of bubble bath.

"No," Mama answered. "We don't need bubble bath. Please put it back."

Next Mama stopped at the hardware store for a pound of nails and a package of picture hooks.

"I want something," said Bumper.

"Not here," Mama answered.

Then Mama wanted to make a quick stop at the pet store. "All we need is fish food," she said firmly.

But Bumper wanted to look at the puppies.

Bonnie wanted to hear the parrot talk.

Becky asked, "Could we get a guinea pig?"

"Not today," Mama answered as she hurried the twins and Bonnie out the door.

Mama had a long list of things to buy at the supermarket. She wanted to get everything on her list, nothing more and nothing less.

The twins ran ahead toward the supermarket door. Becky
got there first. She stepped on the black rubber doormat
with her foot, and the doors opened automatically. Bumper
waited for Mama and Bonnie to come, so he could open
the doors for them.

Mama lifted Bonnie into a shopping cart.

She said, "Bumper, you can push the cart first, then Becky can push it."

"When?" Becky asked. "When will it be *my* turn?"

"Your turn will start in ten minutes," Mama answered. "I'll keep track of the time on my watch."

Bumper liked pushing the cart. Bonnie liked riding in it. Sometimes Bumper pushed the cart ahead, then ran to catch it. Bonnie laughed, but Mama didn't. She told Bumper to hold on to the cart if he wanted to keep pushing.

Mama was busy choosing vegetables.
Bumper was still pushing the cart.

Becky was bored. She squeezed a melon and tasted a grape. She smelled some lemons. She tried to weigh her hand on the scale, but the greengrocer said the scale was just for fruit.

Becky didn't like being told not to touch, so she ran off
to a different aisle.

Becky looked at cereal boxes and cookies and candies and sodas.

She found a big basket of balls and threw one in the air. She made a good catch too.

Then she watched a clerk scoop up a container of salad. Becky tried to read the numbers on the scale, but the clerk took off the container before she could finish.

Just then Becky heard Bonnie crying for a cookie. Becky heard Mama saying, "One cookie, that's all!"

"What can *I* have?" Becky heard Bumper ask.

Becky ran toward them. "And I want something too," she shouted.

Mama looked directly at her children. She said, "You can't have everything you see in a store. Becky, choose something. Bumper, choose something. One good thing to eat—and that's it!"

"And no junk food," added Bumper. "Right?"

"Right!" said Mama. "Twins, meet Bonnie and me near the deli counter in five minutes."

Mama pushed the cart down an aisle stacked with cans—big and small cans, tall and short cans, fat and skinny cans. When Mama stopped to talk to a friend, Bonnie started to kick her feet. She wanted to keep moving.

Mama said, "Stop kicking, Bonnie. A shopping cart is not a swing."

"Let's go," said Bonnie. "Go! Go!"

"In a minute," said Mama. "Look what I have for you—
a book!"

Bonnie smiled when Mama gave her the book to read.
She loved to look at the pictures all by herself.

Mama let Bonnie hold the ticket at the deli counter.
"We're number five," she explained. "We have to wait our
turn."

The counter man flipped the next card. "Four," he called.
"Who's next?"

"Me, me, me," Bonnie yelled back, waving her number.

Mama said, "Bonnie, it's not our turn yet. But soon."

Bumper and Becky came back. Bumper had a bag of pretzel sticks, and Becky had a box of crunchy granola bars.

"Are these good?" they asked Mama.

Mama checked the labels on the packages. "Pretzels have a lot of salt," she said, "but they're okay if you don't eat too many."

"And crunchy bars?"

"Those are fine," answered Mama.

Now it was Becky's turn to push the shopping cart. She pushed it past the pasta, and the cake mixes, and the frozen foods.

"Beep-beep," said Becky when she passed other shopping carts in the aisle.

The shopping cart was almost full. Mama checked her list and said she had everything. It was time to pay.

Bumper and Becky helped unload the cart. Bumper wanted to add a coloring pen. Becky wanted a candy bar. And Bonnie wanted a pack of gum.

Mama glared at all of them. They knew that the answer was no.

Mama put all the groceries in the car. Then she said, "Now all we have to do is buy a birthday present for Cousin Tommy."

"Can we get him a robot?" Becky asked.

"Or a train set?" asked Bumper.

"We'll see," answered Mama.

Inside the toy store Becky said, "Let's get Tommy this," and pointed to a large brown teddy bear.

"No," said Bumper. "I want to get this." He pulled at a box of blocks, and five other boxes almost toppled onto his head.

Becky showed Bonnie a music box with a dancing monkey on top. Bonnie giggled and clapped her hands.

"Can we buy this for Bonnie?" Becky asked.

"We're not here to buy a present for Bonnie—or for you," said Mama. "Try to think of what Tommy would like."

"How?" Becky asked.

"Well," said Mama, "what does Tommy like to do?"

"He likes to read," Bumper answered.

"And paint and draw," added Becky.

"I know!" shouted Bumper. "We can get Tommy this book!"

"And this paint set!" yelled Becky.

"Those are two good ideas," Mama said.

Bumper picked red wrapping paper for the paint set. Becky liked yellow for the book.

"Bonnie can pick the ribbon," said Mama.

And she did!

As she drove toward home Mama asked, "Did you all have a good day?"

"Yes, Mama," said Becky and Bumper.

But Bonnie didn't say a word. She was fast asleep in her car seat.

Bumper gave her a kiss, then almost fell asleep himself. It had been a good shopping day for everyone.